5 STEPS TO A

5

500

AP Microeconomics/
Macroeconomics Questions
to know by test day

Also in the 5 Steps series:

Also in the 500 AP Questions to Know by Test Day series:

5 STEPS TO A >5™

500
AP Microeconomics/
Macroeconomics Questions
to know by test day

Brian Reddington

New York Chicago San Francisco Lisbon London Madrid Mexico City
Milan New Delhi San Juan Seoul Singapore Sydney Toronto

The **McGraw·Hill** Companies

BRIAN REDDINGTON earned his bachelor's degree in history from Stony Brook University in Stony Brook, New York, before pursuing a master's degree in special education at Queens College in New York City. A dedicated educator, he has been teaching economics since 2008. He lives in Bellmore, New York, with his wife and two young daughters, Anna June and Sarah Gretchen.

1 2 3 4 5 6 7 8 9 10 11 12 13 14 15 16 17   QFR/QFR   1 9 8 7 6 5 4 3 2 1

ISBN   978-0-07-177449-9
MHID   0-07-177449-1

e-ISBN   978-0-07-177450-5
e-MHID   0-07-177450-5

Library of Congress Control Number 2011914989

Series interior design by Jane Tennenbaum
Interior illustrations by Cenveo

McGraw-Hill books are available at special quantity discounts to use as premiums and sales promotions or for use in corporate training programs. To contact a representative, please e-mail us at bulksales@mcgraw-hill.com.

This book is printed on acid-free paper.

CONTENTS

INTRODUCTION

Congratulations! You've taken a big step toward AP success by purchasing *5 Steps to a 5: 500 AP Microeconomics/Macroeconomics Questions to Know by Test Day*. We are here to help you take the next step and score high on your AP exam so you can earn college credits and get into the college or university of your choice.

This book gives you 500 AP-style multiple-choice questions that cover all the most essential course material. Each question has a detailed answer explanation. These questions will give you valuable independent practice to supplement your regular textbook and the groundwork you are already doing in your AP classroom. This and the other books in this series were written by expert AP teachers who know your exam inside out and can identify the crucial exam information as well as questions that are most likely to appear on the exam.

You might be the kind of student who takes several AP courses and needs to study extra questions a few weeks before the exam for a final review. Or you might be the kind of student who puts off preparing until the last weeks before the exam. No matter what your preparation style is, you will surely benefit from reviewing these 500 questions, which closely parallel the content, format, and degree of difficulty of the questions on the actual AP exam. These questions and their answer explanations are the ideal last-minute study tool for those final few weeks before the test.

Remember the old saying "Practice makes perfect." If you practice with all the questions and answers in this book, we are certain you will build the skills and confidence you need to do great on the exam. Good luck!

—Editors of McGraw-Hill Education

Microeconomics

CHAPTER 1

Basic Economic Concepts

1. The study of economics is correctly defined as
    (A) the methods used to satisfy our limited material wants with unlimited productive resources
    (B) how best to predict the fluctuations in the stock market
    (C) how best to satisfy our unlimited wants with limited and scarce material resources
    (D) the methods used to disseminate limited resources among a population's scarce material wants
    (E) the study of the interaction and allocation of limited resources and market structures

2. Deirdre has one free hour to practice the piano for an upcoming school concert or work at the library for $7 per hour or babysit her neighbor's 12-year-old son for $10 per hour. She chooses to practice the piano. What is the opportunity cost of practicing the piano?
    (A) The opportunity cost would be $17 because she chose not to participate in these activities.
    (B) Without knowing the marginal value of practicing the piano, there is no way of knowing the true opportunity cost.
    (C) The opportunity cost would be $20 because it is necessary to calculate one additional hour of babysitting to make it profitable.
    (D) The opportunity cost would be $10 because it would be the most profitable alternative.
    (E) The opportunity cost would be $3 because it is the monetary difference between two alternative choices.

3. After dedicating two hours to studying for the AP economics exam, Seth chooses to spend an additional hour studying. Which of the following is most likely TRUE?

    (A) The marginal benefit of the additional hour is at least as great as the marginal cost of the additional hour.
    (B) The marginal cost of the additional hour is less than the marginal benefit of the additional hour.
    (C) Both the marginal benefit and marginal cost are always equal in this scenario.
    (D) The marginal benefit of the second hour is less than the marginal benefit of the additional hour.
    (E) The marginal cost of the second hour is greater than the marginal cost of the additional hour.

Brooks Industries is a leading producer of guitars and stereos. Use the following production possibilities curve for questions 4 and 5.

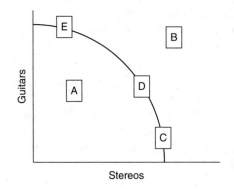

4. Which two points would best represent economic growth?

    (A) From A to D
    (B) From D to C
    (C) From A to B
    (D) From E to C
    (E) From E to B

5. The concave shape of the production possibilities curve implies the notion of

    (A) opportunity costs
    (B) comparative advantage
    (C) marginal analysis
    (D) allocation of limited resources with unlimited material wants
    (E) MB = MC

6. It is beneficial for two countries to trade only when there is
   (A) a mutually beneficial trade agreement
   (B) increasing returns to scale
   (C) decreasing returns to scale
   (D) an absolute advantage in production between the two countries
   (E) a comparative advantage in production between the two countries

7. If a society *overallocates* its resources, then
   (A) consumer spending would increase due to an increase in demand
   (B) marginal benefit would be greater than marginal cost
   (C) opportunity cost of producing one more unit would increase exponentially
   (D) marginal benefit would be less than marginal cost
   (E) marginal benefit would equal marginal cost

8. Both Richard and Michele can mow the lawn and walk their dog on Sunday morning. For every half hour of walking the dog, Richard can mow twice the amount of lawn Michele can. According to this information,
   (A) Michele walks the dog because she has absolute advantage in mowing the lawn
   (B) Richard walks the dog because he has comparative advantage in mowing the lawn
   (C) Richard mows the lawn because he has comparative advantage in mowing the lawn
   (D) Michele mows the lawn because she has comparative advantage in mowing the lawn
   (E) Michele walks the dog because she has comparative advantage in walking the dog

9. In a command economy,
   (A) market prices are determined through supply and demand
   (B) market prices are determined through supply and demand and some government interventions
   (C) market prices are determined by a central plan designed by the government
   (D) market prices are determined through supply and demand and some barter system
   (E) market prices are determined through the resources backing of the gold and silver supply

10. Which of the following will cause an outward shift of the production possibilities curve?
    (A) A grant for educational training for employees
    (B) A decrease in a nation's birthrate, thus decreasing the labor force
    (C) A natural disaster creating extreme limitations of a vital natural resource
    (D) A shortage of skilled workers
    (E) An increase of unskilled workers

11. A point lying directly on the production possibilities curve is
    (A) efficient
    (B) unattainable, yet efficient
    (C) attainable and efficient
    (D) unattainable
    (E) inefficient

12. *Scarcity* is best defined as
    (A) material resources are unlimited
    (B) an idea used by industrializing nations to satisfy unlimited wants and desires with limited natural resources
    (C) limited vital material resources compared with limited wants and needs
    (D) all points lying outside the production possibilities curve
    (E) the idea that a society's wants and needs are unlimited, and material resources are limited

13. The benefits of specialization likely include all of the following EXCEPT
    (A) vital resources are used more efficiently
    (B) an increased educational opportunity as the economy grows
    (C) improvements in productivity
    (D) greater quantity of goods and services supplied to consumers
    (E) all of the above are benefits of specialization

14. Mineral deposits, human capital, entrepreneurship, and use of technology and machinery are all examples of
    (A) factors of production
    (B) superior and inferior goods
    (C) elements sometimes needed to move an existing company overseas
    (D) public goods
    (E) material wants and needs

15. The law of increasing costs is best defined as
- (A) when the price of a good rises, the quantity does not fall
- (B) as more of a product is produced, the greater its opportunity cost
- (C) as one obtains more of a good, the marginal utility (the value from one more unit) will decrease
- (D) as the economy grows, government spending will increase as well
- (E) all costs are opportunity costs

16. The production possibilities curve will show a straight line if which of the following are TRUE?
- (A) Resources are not specialized.
- (B) Vital resources for the good are limitless.
- (C) The economy is operating below maximum efficiency and output.
- (D) The law of decreasing marginal utility does not apply.
- (E) Marginal benefit is less than marginal cost.

17. A country is said to have a comparative advantage over another country when
- (A) it can produce a good at a lower opportunity cost than another country
- (B) it can produce a good using fewer resources per unit of output than another country
- (C) there is a higher degree of specialization and division of labor compared to another country
- (D) when comparing each country's production possibilities frontiers, one country is operating at maximum efficiency and output
- (E) one country's production possibilities frontier is shifted farther to the right compared to another country's production possibilities frontier

18. How is it possible for a country to obtain more than its production possibilities curve dictates?
- (A) Not possible without greater quantities of the factors of production already obtained
- (B) Specialization
- (C) Increase in education and job training
- (D) Obtainment of a greater quantity of affordable substitutes
- (E) Increase in the division of labor

19. Suppose both Spain and Germany produce soccer balls and golf balls. Spain can produce soccer balls at a lower opportunity cost than Germany. Germany can produce golf balls at a lower opportunity cost than Spain. According to the law of comparative advantage,

    (A) Germany should stop producing soccer balls; Spain should stop producing golf balls; Spain and Germany should establish a trade for the product they stopped producing
    (B) Germany should stop producing golf balls; Spain should stop producing soccer balls
    (C) Germany should increase production of golf balls and decrease the production of soccer balls
    (D) Spain should increase the production of soccer balls and decrease the production of golf balls
    (E) none of the above

20. Which of the following are some of the basic questions every economy must answer?

    (A) What to produce? How to produce? How much to produce?
    (B) When to produce? How to produce? How much to produce?
    (C) For whom to produce? When to produce? What to produce?
    (D) What to produce? How to produce? Where to produce?
    (E) all of the above

21. Economic growth is only possible if

    (A) all of the fundamental questions an economy faces are answered
    (B) there is a highly developed division of labor
    (C) there is a decrease in resources and decreasing opportunity costs
    (D) there is an increase in resources and technological advancements in production
    (E) there is a diseconomy of scale

22. As a rule, one should purchase a good or engage in an activity if

    (A) the opportunity cost is equal to the value of the good or activity
    (B) the marginal benefit is greater or equal to the marginal cost
    (C) the value of a good or activity is equal to the marginal cost
    (D) there is an increasing marginal value of return
    (E) the marginal benefit is less than or equal to the marginal cost

23. Your school decides to build a new performing arts center. What is the opportunity cost of the performing arts center?
    (A) The money used in construction of the performing arts center
    (B) The cost of building the performing arts center now rather than waiting until next year
    (C) Any other good or service that cannot be provided right now due to resources used for the new performing arts center
    (D) Cannot be determined without knowing what the next best option was for using the resources that went to the performing arts center
    (E) None of the above

24. All are reasons why a production possibilities curve will shift to the right EXCEPT
    (A) the quantity of resources increases
    (B) the quality of existing resources increases
    (C) technological advancements in production
    (D) the labor force increases
    (E) the economy is operating at allocative efficiency

25. Marginal analysis is best defined as
    (A) the additional benefit received from the consumption of the next unit of a good or service
    (B) the additional cost from the consumption of the next unit of a good or service
    (C) analyzing the combination of goods and services that provide the best benefit to society
    (D) making decisions based upon the marginal benefits and marginal costs of that decision
    (E) when businesses use their resources to produce goods and services for which they have a comparative advantage

26. An economic system is characterized as emphasizing private property and competition, and prices inform buyers and sellers how to allocate their resources. This economic system would be known as a
    (A) mixed system
    (B) market system
    (C) socialist system
    (D) command system
    (E) barter system

27. Economic systems differ most in
    (A) increasing returns to scale
    (B) the quality of goods and services produced
    (C) how they answer the fundamental economic questions all societies must answer
    (D) production possibility frontiers
    (E) the quantity of goods and services produced

28. As a result of the scarcity of resources,
    (A) every society must commit to central planning
    (B) the government must decide how best to use those resources
    (C) there is the unavoidable reality of poverty
    (D) every society must choose how best to use those resources
    (E) every society must include elements of a market economy and government planning

29. All of the following are microeconomic variables EXCEPT
    (A) the unemployment rate from Great Britain in 1992
    (B) tax rates on cigarettes and alcohol in France between 2000 and 2010
    (C) the production possibilities frontier of television sets and radios in Sri Lanka in 1975
    (D) marginal analysis
    (E) all of the above are microeconomic variables

30. The basic economic questions being answered by the decisions of buyers and sellers in the marketplace occur in
    (A) a mixed economy
    (B) a command economy
    (C) a traditional economy
    (D) a market economy
    (E) a barter economy

CHAPTER 2

The Nature and Function of Product Markets

31. What will most likely result if the price of apples decreases?

(A) The quantity of apples demanded will increase.
(B) The supply of apples will decrease.
(C) The demand for apples will increase.
(D) The quantity of apples supplied will decrease.
(E) None of the above

32. If Michael's average yearly income increases, and it is observed that his demand for steak has increased, then steak must be considered

(A) an inferior good
(B) a normal good
(C) a determinant of demand
(D) a determinant of supply
(E) a necessity

33. If Peter's average yearly income increases, and it is observed that his demand for thrift-store-bought shoes decreases, then thrift-store-bought shoes must be considered

(A) a normal good
(B) a shortage good
(C) a necessity
(D) an inferior good
(E) a determinant of demand

34. Suppose it is necessary for tin to be used in the production of guitar strings. If the price of tin decreases and all other variables are constant, what will most likely result?

    (A) The demand for silver will increase.
    (B) The quantity demanded for guitars will decrease.
    (C) The demand for guitars will increase.
    (D) The supply of guitars will decrease.
    (E) The supply of guitar strings will increase.

35. According to the law of demand,

    (A) as the price of a good or service increases, the demand will shift to the right
    (B) as the price of a good or service increases, the demand will shift to the left
    (C) there is an inverse relationship between quantity demanded of a good or service and the price of that good or service
    (D) as prices for a good or service increase, consumers will begin to use substitute goods
    (E) as the price of a good or service increases, the quantity demanded will increase

36. According to the law of supply,

    (A) as the price of a good or service decrease, the supply will decrease
    (B) as the price of a good or service increases, the quantity supplied will increase
    (C) as the price of a good or service increases, the quantity demanded will increase
    (D) as the price of a good or service increases, the quantity demanded will decrease
    (E) there is an inverse relationship between the price of a good or service and the quantity supplied

37. Within the market system, prices are determined by

    (A) supply and demand
    (B) the determinants of supply and demand
    (C) opportunity cost
    (D) total market demand
    (E) production costs

38. A hurricane destroys a significant supply of bananas in 2011. As a result, the price of bananas increases. What prediction may be made regarding the supply of apples, a substitute good, when its market is in equilibrium?

(A) The price rises, and the supply will increase.
(B) The quantity supplied will increase.
(C) The price falls, and the supply will decrease.
(D) The price falls, and the quantity supplied will decrease.
(E) Both the price and the quantity supplied are undetermined.

39. Competition in a market system best helps a society because

(A) supply and demand establish the best price for a good or service
(B) all opportunity costs are heavily analyzed
(C) the total welfare is increased
(D) aggregate supply and aggregate demand are balanced
(E) within the production possibilities frontier, all resources are maximized and used efficiently

40. If the demand for tennis rackets increases, what prediction can be made regarding tennis balls?

(A) The demand for tennis balls will fall.
(B) The supply for tennis balls will remain the same.
(C) The price of tennis balls will remain the same.
(D) The quantity supply for tennis balls will fall.
(E) The price and the quantity supply of tennis balls will increase.

41. Which of the following situations will cause the demand curve for chicken, a normal good, to shift to the left?

(A) Consumer incomes decrease.
(B) Consumer incomes increase.
(C) The price of steak decreases.
(D) There is a decrease in the cost of raising chickens on a farm.
(E) There is a scientific discovery that relates eating chicken to lower blood pressure.

42. Which of the following refers to an indifference curve?

(A) A curve that illustrates the levels of utility or satisfaction for a consumer when he or she is presented with a various combination of goods
(B) An inverse relationship between quantity demanded and price
(C) A direct relationship between quantity demanded and price
(D) A direct relationship between quantity supplied and price
(E) None of the above

43. Mr. Harrington produces hot dog buns. He is most likely to sell his hot dog buns at a higher price if
(A) the price of hot dogs decreases
(B) there is an increase in consumer income
(C) the price of hot dogs increases
(D) a new technology is developed enabling an increase in hot dog production
(E) a new technology is developed enabling an increase in hot dog bun production

44. The equilibrium price is established
(A) at the next price above where the demand and supply curves intersect
(B) when the quantity supplied equals the quantity demanded
(C) at the next price below where the demand and supply curves intersect
(D) when you take the difference between the two lowest points plotted on the demand and supply curves
(E) at the price where either the demand or supply curve becomes horizontal

Observe the following demand curve for baseballs to answer question 45.

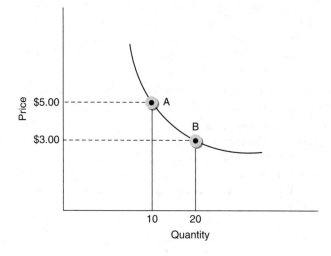

45. Which of the following could explain the movement from point B to point A?

(A) An increase in the price of the good
(B) An increase in consumer income
(C) An increase in the price of a complementary good
(D) An increase in the price of a substitute good
(E) None of the above

46. Doherty Industries is a leading producer of an energy drink. Which of the following will cause Doherty Industries to offer more of the product at all possible sale prices?

(A) A competitor lowers the price of the product.
(B) The price of a key ingredient increases.
(C) The price of a key ingredient decreases.
(D) The demand for the energy drink decreases.
(E) The demand is perfectly elastic.

47. Suppose the demand for a product is inelastic. If a producer wishes to increase total revenue, he or she should

(A) decrease prices
(B) decrease the quantity supplied
(C) increase the quantity supplied
(D) expand production into the global market
(E) raise prices

48. Which is an important factor to make the demand for a good inelastic?

(A) It is a necessity.
(B) There are many substitutes.
(C) It is a luxury item.
(D) There are many cross-price substitutes.
(E) A significant portion of consumers' budgets goes to purchasing the good.

49. There is a 10% rise in the price of bottled water. This creates a 40% change in the quantity demanded. The demand for bottled water is considered to be

(A) perfectly inelastic
(B) elastic
(C) inelastic
(D) perfectly elastic
(E) none of the above

50. If a 30% rise in gas prices creates a 0% decrease in the quantity demanded, the demand is said to be
    (A) inelastic
    (B) perfectly elastic
    (C) elastic
    (D) perfectly inelastic
    (E) none of the above

51. All of the following are factors affecting the elasticity of demand EXCEPT
    (A) availability of substitute goods
    (B) necessity versus luxury goods
    (C) how much of a consumer's budget goes to the good
    (D) the time horizon in which a change in price is considered
    (E) the percentage change in the quantity demanded

Use the following graph to answer questions 52 and 53.

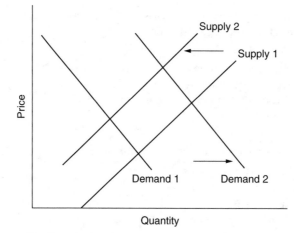

52. All of the following are factors that contributed to Demand 1 shifting to Demand 2 EXCEPT
    (A) an increase in consumer income
    (B) a decrease in price of a substitute good
    (C) an increase in the number of buyers in a market
    (D) consumers expect the price of the good to increase in the future
    (E) the product's popularity with consumers increased

53. All of the following are factors that contributed to Supply 1 shifting to Supply 2 EXCEPT
    (A) the price of a key ingredient to the product decreased
    (B) the number of sellers decreased
    (C) sellers expect the price of the good to rise in the future
    (D) the government increased a tax on the product
    (E) the product is no longer subsidized by the government

54. A price ceiling is usually set
    (A) above the equilibrium price and quantity
    (B) at the intersection of the supply and demand curves
    (C) by subtracting the highest price for supply and the lowest point for demand on their respective curves
    (D) below the equilibrium price
    (E) none of the above

55. Which factor contributes to price elasticity of supply?
    (A) Time
    (B) Inflexibility of sellers
    (C) Consumer expectations regarding future prices
    (D) Producer tastes and preferences
    (E) The availability of a producer surplus

56. Consumer surplus is measured by
    (A) the area to the right of the supply curve but below the price equilibrium
    (B) the sum of buyer and seller surplus
    (C) the area above the supply curve but below the price equilibrium
    (D) the quotient of percentage change in quantity supplied and percentage change in price
    (E) the quotient of percentage change in quantity demanded and percentage change in price

57. All of the following would influence the position of the demand curve for golf clubs EXCEPT
    (A) the price of golf clubs
    (B) the price of golf balls
    (C) the price of golf shoes
    (D) the size of the population
    (E) A and C

58. If the supply curve remains constant, an increase in demand will cause

(A) an increase in prices and a larger quantity sold
(B) an increase in prices and a smaller quantity sold
(C) a decrease in prices and a larger quantity sold
(D) a decrease in prices and a smaller quantity sold
(E) none of the above

59. A price increase in Product X resulted in an increase in demand for Product Z. Product Z is most likely a(n)

(A) inferior good
(B) complementary good
(C) substitute good
(D) normal good
(E) factor of production

60. A limit on interest rates charged by a credit card company is an example of a

(A) price floor
(B) price ceiling
(C) price support
(D) consequence of minimum wage law
(E) negative externality

61. When quantity demanded is greater than quantity supplied, there is a(n)

(A) negative externality
(B) shortage in the market
(C) surplus in the market
(D) increase in government regulation
(E) decrease in unemployment

62. If the price of a good increases, the most likely result would be for the

(A) quantity supplied to increase
(B) quantity supplied to decrease
(C) demand to increase
(D) supply to decrease
(E) demand to decrease

63. The notion that the actions of producers in their own self-interest will result to further the public interest is known as

(A) the invisible hand
(B) consumer sovereignty
(C) the law of demand
(D) derived demand
(E) none of the above

64. Price, technology, taxes, and the number of producers in an industry are known as

(A) factors of production
(B) capital and human capital
(C) producer expectations
(D) determinants of supply
(E) determinants of demand

65. Another name for *excess supply* is

(A) disequilibrium
(B) equilibrium point
(C) Gini ratio
(D) surplus
(E) shortage

66. Establishing an effective price floor would help

(A) reduce a surplus
(B) increase a surplus
(C) remove the need for government regulation
(D) decrease demand
(E) increase government regulation

Use the following diagram to answer question 67.

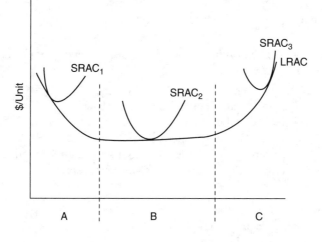

67. Sections A, B, and C of the preceding short-run and long-run average cost graph show, respectively,
    (A) economies of scale, constant returns to scale, and diseconomies of scale
    (B) economies of scale, diseconomies of scale, and constant returns to scale
    (C) diseconomies of scale, constant returns to scale, and economies of scale
    (D) diseconomies of scale, economies of scale, and constant returns to scale
    (E) constant returns to scale, economies of scale, and diseconomies of scale

68. The number of substitutes for a good and time are known as
    (A) determinants of supply
    (B) determinants of demand
    (C) determinants of elasticity
    (D) factors of production
    (E) elements of the Gini ratio

69. If the price of cigarettes increases, we would expect
    (A) demand to be inelastic
    (B) demand to be elastic
    (C) government regulation of the industry to decrease
    (D) government regulation of the industry to increase
    (E) many producers to exit the market

70. Suppose the price of iPhones increases 2% and the quantity demanded for iPhones decreases by 4%, then
    (A) elasticity is 2 and demand is price elastic
    (B) elasticity is 0.5 and demand is price inelastic
    (C) elasticity is 8 and demand is price elastic
    (D) elasticity is .05 and demand is price inelastic
    (E) answer cannot be determined without knowing the length of time the product is on the market with the increase in price

71. A surplus would be found
    (A) below the equilibrium point
    (B) above the equilibrium point
    (C) in the top portion of the upward sloping supply curve
    (D) in the bottom portion of the upward sloping supply curve
    (E) none of the above

72. Suppose the market is in equilibrium for razor blades where the marginal benefit equals the marginal cost. If the government imposes a tax on razor blades and the marginal cost is greater than the marginal benefit, what may result?
    (A) Dead weight loss
    (B) An increase in demand
    (C) An increase in supply
    (D) A price ceiling
    (E) A price floor

73. Dead weight loss refers to
    (A) the lost benefit to society caused by the movement away from the market equilibrium
    (B) the gained benefit to suppliers caused by the increase in the market equilibrium
    (C) the incremental benefit or loss when the consumer increases consumption by one additional unit (marginal utility)
    (D) the legal maximum price above which a product cannot be sold (price ceiling)
    (E) the legal minimum price below which a product cannot be sold (price floor)

74. The law of diminishing marginal utility refers to
    (A) the marginal utility from consuming one additional item will fall
    (B) the marginal utility from consuming one additional item will increase
    (C) marginal benefit should equal marginal cost in a market
    (D) MC > MB when the market is in disequilibrium
    (E) price floors help establish MB > MC

75. If you calculate the elasticity of a good to be less than 0, you are correct to assume
    (A) it is a normal good
    (B) it is a luxury good
    (C) people will buy the good regardless of the price
    (D) the good has few substitutes
    (E) the good has few complements

76. What percentage of the business firms in the United States are sole proprietorships?

   (A) 5%
   (B) 15%
   (C) 25%
   (D) 55%
   (E) 75%

77. The difference between the interests of owners and managers in a firm would be considered what kind of problem?

   (A) principal-agent problem
   (B) free-rider problem
   (C) limited liability problem
   (D) marginal utility problem
   (E) rationing problem

78. The idea of limited liability is a significant factor to which type of business organization?

   (A) Sole proprietorships
   (B) Monopolies
   (C) Corporations
   (D) Partnerships
   (E) All of the above

79. If a business owns plants at various stages of production, this is known as

   (A) a vertically integrated firm
   (B) a multiplant firm
   (C) a conglomerate
   (D) a sole proprietorship
   (E) an oligopoly

80. A government policy to tax producers is the possible result of

   (A) spillover costs
   (B) positive externalities
   (C) principal-agent problem
   (D) free-rider problem
   (E) all of the above

81. A business organization that operates and owns multiple plants is known as a(n)

(A) industry
(B) franchise
(C) partnership
(D) oligopoly
(E) firm

82. The best way a government deals with a monopoly is by

(A) creating a competing firm that is government owned
(B) creating regulations on the monopoly firm
(C) redistributing a percentage of the monopoly's profit through specific tax laws
(D) compensating firms hurt by the power of the monopoly
(E) A, B, and C

83. A monopolistic competition refers to

(A) extensive economies of scale and higher cost-efficiency when there is only one firm for the entire demand of a product
(B) a few small firms offering a differentiated product with easy entry into the market
(C) a market structure with a small number of interdependent large firms producing a standardized product
(D) the most competitive market structure
(E) the least competitive market structure

84. An oligopoly refers to

(A) extensive economies of scale and higher cost-efficiency when there is only one firm for the entire demand of a product
(B) the least competitive market structure
(C) a market structure with a small number of interdependent large firms producing a standardized product
(D) a few small firms offering a differentiated product with easy entry into the market
(E) the most competitive market structure

85. A monopoly refers to

  (A) the least competitive market structure
  (B) the most competitive market structure
  (C) a market structure with a small number of interdependent large firms producing a standardized product
  (D) extensive economies of scale and higher cost-efficiency when there is only one firm for the entire demand of a product
  (E) the most competitive market structure

86. A perfect competition refers to

  (A) the most competitive market structure
  (B) the least competitive market structure
  (C) extensive economies of scale and higher cost-efficiency when there is only one firm for the entire demand of a product
  (D) a few small firms offering a differentiated product with easy entry into the market
  (E) a market structure with a small number of interdependent large firms producing a standardized product

87. The difference between a monopoly and a monopolistic competition is

  (A) differentiated products
  (B) monopolies exist due to extensive economies of scale
  (C) accessibility of entry into the market
  (D) government regulation
  (E) the size of the market

88. No barriers to entry or exit, many firms, and a standardized product are characteristics of which type of market structure?

  (A) Monopolistic competition
  (B) Oligopoly
  (C) Natural monopoly
  (D) Monopoly
  (E) Perfect competition

89. The services of natural gas, water, and electricity brought into the household are best consigned to which market structure?

  (A) Monopolistic competition
  (B) Oligopoly
  (C) Perfect competition
  (D) Natural monopoly
  (E) Monopoly

Use the following diagram to answer questions 90 and 91.

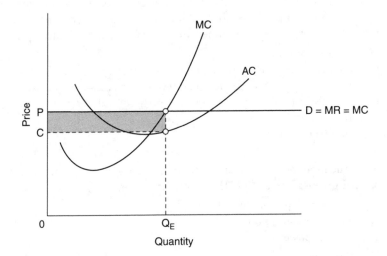

90. The preceding diagram represents which type of market structure?
   (A) Monopolistic competition
   (B) Perfect competition
   (C) Natural monopoly
   (D) Monopoly
   (E) Oligopoly

91. At which point is the graph showing profit maximization?
   (A) MR = MC
   (B) AC = P
   (C) MC = AC
   (D) The area between MC and AC
   (E) It is not showing profit maximization.

92. What is the most likely reason perfectly competitive firms do not make a profit in the long run?
   (A) Barriers of exit from the market
   (B) The product being standardized with little differentiation
   (C) The arrival of new firms on the market
   (D) The firms being "price takers"
   (E) All of the above

93. Suppose you pick up the latest edition of *The Economist* and read that Company Z, a producer of cigarettes, recently purchased 8 out of the 10 biggest farms that produce tobacco. Since you are a very good AP Economics student, you realize immediately that Company Z is attempting to

(A) increase profits
(B) establish an oligopoly through collusive pricing
(C) maximize profits where marginal revenue equals marginal cost
(D) establish a monopoly through a majority control of a factor of production
(E) none of the above

94. Since the monopolist has many barriers to entry and no competition, he or she has price-setting ability. This is also known as

(A) purchasing power
(B) profit maximization
(C) market power
(D) efficiency
(E) none of the above

95. A monopolistic competition has some market power because

(A) overall, there are not many competitors
(B) overall, it has a large number of competitors
(C) the government restricts the use of patents for monopolistic competitors through antitrust legislation
(D) advertising allows monopolistic competitors to set any price they wish
(E) none of the above

96. Imagine a perfectly competitive market. If the market price of the product is $15 and the marginal cost is also $15, which of the following is true?

(A) The firm is making zero profit.
(B) Many firms will soon leave the market.
(C) Many firms will join together to increase profit through collusive pricing.
(D) The firm is profit maximizing.
(E) All of the above

97. For a perfectly competitive market, the best way to maximize profit is

(A) $MR = MC$
(B) $MRP < W$
(C) $AFC = MB$
(D) $MC > MB$
(E) none of the above

98. If a firm owns a patent on a product, what may occur?

(A) A monopoly

(B) An oligopoly

(C) A cartel

(D) The firm becomes price takers.

(E) The firm may maximize profits at MC = MR.

99. A monopoly might come into existence if

(A) there are economies of scale

(B) there are no economies of scale

(C) there is price discrimination

(D) a firm is a price taker

(E) A and B

100. Economies of scale refers to

(A) a decrease in efficiency of production as the number of goods produced increases

(B) an increase in efficiency of production as the number of goods produced increases

(C) an increase in efficiency of production as the number of goods produced decreases

(D) a firm maximizing profit through dominance of the market

(E) sensitivity to the determinants of supply and demand and price level

101. Product differentiation is an essential part of which type of market structure?

(A) Oligopoly

(B) Monopoly

(C) Monopolistic competition

(D) Natural monopoly

(E) Perfect competition

102. One of the key differences the makers of the iPhones and the BlackBerry smartphones utilize as part of a monopolistic competition is

(A) product differentiation

(B) patents

(C) limited liability

(D) licenses

(E) game theory

103. All of the following are examples of production inputs adjustable in the short run EXCEPT

(A) the amount of wood and glass to construct a window
(B) the size of the garage in an auto-repair shop
(C) the ratio of raisins to cornflakes in a breakfast cereal
(D) the number of custodians working in a local high school
(E) the amount of gas heat consumed in a household

104. If marginal cost falls in the beginning and then gradually rises as output increases, you would know that

(A) the law of diminishing returns is valid
(B) MC = MB
(C) this market structure is a perfect competition
(D) this market structure is a monopolistic competition
(E) you would have a constant returns to scale

105. All of the following are variable production inputs EXCEPT

(A) the amount of electricity used in a plant
(B) the total amount of raw materials utilized in a plant
(C) human capital
(D) the size of a firm's labor force
(E) all of the above are variable production inputs

106. If the price of a variable resource increases, the result would be

(A) a downward shift of MC
(B) an upward shift in AFC
(C) an upward shift in MC
(D) a downward shift in ATC
(E) an upward shift in MP

107. Businesses are required by law to set prices either on or relatively close to the costs that firms incurred to make the good or service. This idea is known as

(A) the average cost pricing rule
(B) the ability to pay rule
(C) an antitrust law
(D) law of diminishing marginal returns
(E) economies of scale

108. The key difference between the short run and the long run is that the short run
    (A) cannot change the size of the plant
    (B) is enough time to change the size of the plant
    (C) is enough time to change the amount of capital
    (D) is not enough time to change the amount of raw materials
    (E) A, B, and C

109. The difference between total revenue and total explicit and implicit costs is known as
    (A) economic profit
    (B) accounting profit
    (C) total fixed costs
    (D) total variable costs
    (E) total costs

110. As a result of increased growth, a firm may experience difficulty in managing larger plants and may lose efficiency. This is known as
    (A) constant returns to scale
    (B) explicit costs
    (C) law of diminishing marginal returns
    (D) diseconomies of scale
    (E) economies of scale

111. If the long-run average cost curve is constant over a variety of plant sizes, this is known as
    (A) diseconomies of scale
    (B) economies of scale
    (C) explicit costs
    (D) law of diminishing marginal returns
    (E) constant returns to scale

112. Specialization and lower costs of inputs will often result in
    (A) a decrease in economic profits
    (B) economies of scale
    (C) a decrease in implicit costs
    (D) constant returns to scale
    (E) diseconomies of scale

113. An organization that employs factors of production to produce a good or
service is known as a

(A) monopoly
(B) natural monopoly
(C) firm
(D) partnership
(E) limited liability corporation

Use the following graph to answer question 114.

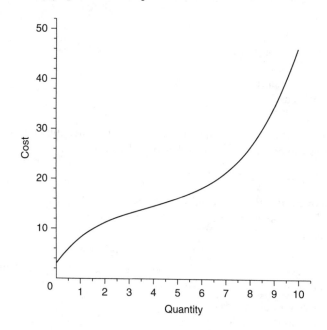

114. The preceding graph shows

(A) a total cost curve
(B) a total revenue curve
(C) no increasing returns in the early stage of production
(D) a fixed variable cost curve
(E) no diminishing returns

115. Mr. Ray is a business owner of a competitive firm. He is trying to decide whether to shut down his firm in the short run. Which factors should Mr. Ray analyze to help in his decision?

(A) Average variable cost and marginal revenue
(B) Total revenue and total cost
(C) Total fixed cost and total revenue
(D) Price and average total cost
(E) Price and marginal benefit

116. All of the following are part of a monopolistic competition market structure EXCEPT

(A) differentiated products
(B) dead weight loss
(C) profits in the short run
(D) patents
(E) all of the above are part of a monopolistic competition market structure

117. In a perfect competition, if P > ATC, which of the following will take place in the long run?

(A) Price decreases as more firms exit the market.
(B) Price decreases as more firms enter the market.
(C) Price increases as more firms enter the market.
(D) Profits decrease as price increases.
(E) None of the above

118. Richard and Michelle enjoy going to the museum. During the month of April, the museum is exhibiting works on 20th-century feminism and is offering the admission price to women as half off. Richard must pay full price for admission. This is an example of

(A) dead weight loss
(B) variable costs
(C) price discrimination
(D) market power
(E) sex discrimination

119. Dead weight loss occurs in which type of market structure?

(A) Oligopoly
(B) Monopolistic competition
(C) Monopoly
(D) Perfect competition
(E) A, B, and C

120. If prices fall below AVC, what should a firm decide to do?

(A) Differentiate products
(B) Raise prices
(C) Cut TFC
(D) Lay off workers
(E) Shut down

121. The profit-maximizing rule states that to maximize profits a firm should produce where

(A) $MR = MC$
(B) $MR > MC$
(C) $MR < MC$
(D) $MB > MC$
(E) $MB = MC$

122. When there is zero incentive for more firms to enter a perfectly competitive market, it is said that the market has reached

(A) constant returns to scale
(B) economies of scale
(C) diseconomies of scale
(D) long-run equilibrium
(E) none of the above

123. If new firms enter the market, what is most likely to occur?

(A) The cost curve will shift upward.
(B) Total revenue will increase.
(C) The cost curve will shift downward.
(D) Market power decreases.
(E) None of the above

124. Cartels are an example of
- (A) a perfect competition
- (B) a monopolistic competition
- (C) collusive pricing
- (D) the best way to use dominant strategy
- (E) the prisoner's dilemma

125. Few large producers, barriers to entry, and mutual interdependence are characteristics of a(n)
- (A) perfect competition
- (B) monopolistic competition
- (C) oligopoly
- (D) monopoly
- (E) natural monopoly

126. Why is the demand for fruit less price elastic than the demand for a boat?
- (A) Consumption of fruit is greater.
- (B) A boat is an inferior good.
- (C) There are more suppliers of fruit than boat manufacturers.
- (D) Fruit takes up less of a consumer's budget.
- (E) All of the above

127. All of the following are long-run production decisions EXCEPT
- (A) an auto-repair shop decides to increase the size of its garage
- (B) a school decides to hire more teaching assistants due to an increase in the school population
- (C) a firm increases the number of its plants
- (D) a school decides to add more classrooms and a new performing arts center
- (E) a firm decides to close 5% of its plants

128. More firms entering a market, a decrease in price, and a decrease in long-run profits are a result of
- (A) several firms earning an economic profit on a good or service
- (B) the characteristics of monopolistic competition
- (C) the characteristics of an oligopoly
- (D) several firms not earning an economic profit on a good or service in the short run
- (E) the prisoner's dilemma

129. Danielle decides to withdraw her savings of $70,000 and invest in starting her own clothing business. She normally earns $3,000 in interest from her savings. If Danielle earned an accounting profit of $60,000 last year, what was her economic profit?

(A) $10,000
(B) $7,000
(C) $13,000
(D) $60,000
(E) $57,000

130. Firm X decides to shut down production in the short run where its costs would be

(A) AVC only
(B) AVC and TFC only
(C) TFC only
(D) zero
(E) none of the above

131. If a monopoly and a perfect competition have the same costs, the monopoly will always

(A) charge a lesser price than the perfect competition
(B) produce the same quantity as the perfect competition
(C) charge a higher price than the perfect competition and produce less
(D) charge a higher price than the perfect competition and produce more
(E) none of the above

132. The U-shaped average cost curve is a reality for most business firms because

(A) firms experience diseconomies of scales in the long run
(B) firms experience economies of scale in the short run
(C) firms experience economies of scale and then diseconomies of scale
(D) firms experience only constant returns to scale
(E) none of the above

133. The market for smartphones may be considered a monopolistic competition rather than a perfect competition because

(A) there is product differentiation
(B) there is no product differentiation
(C) profits in the long run decrease as more firms enter the market
(D) they are price takers
(E) all of the above

134. If the quantity supplied equals the quantity demanded for a good or service, it is said that

  (A) there is a surplus for a perfectly competitive market
  (B) the market is in equilibrium for a perfect competition
  (C) the market is in equilibrium for an oligopoly
  (D) the market is in equilibrium for a monopoly
  (E) all of the above

135. If the price of cigarettes is in equilibrium, what is needed to increase the price?

  (A) Consumer income to decrease
  (B) Consumer expectations to remain the same
  (C) The price of tobacco to increase
  (D) The government to decrease regulations
  (E) The price of tobacco to decrease

136. Consumer surplus is the

  (A) difference between the price consumers would have been willing to pay and the price they actually did pay
  (B) price consumers would have been willing to pay minus total variable costs
  (C) price consumers would have been willing to pay in addition to total variable costs
  (D) price consumers would have been willing to pay in addition to total fixed costs
  (E) price consumers would have been willing to pay minus total fixed and variable costs

137. If you are reading a firm's business plan and see many resources dedicated to advertising, you would know that the firm's market structure is a(n)

  (A) oligopoly
  (B) natural monopoly
  (C) monopoly
  (D) perfect competition
  (E) monopolistic competition

138. It's Theresa's first trip to New York City. She goes and sees all the sights and finds herself walking through Times Square. She looks up and sees two billboards for the iPad and the BlackBerry tablet. Since Theresa is an excellent AP Economics student, she immediately realizes that these two different companies are

- (A) monopolistic competition because of product differentiation and extensive advertising
- (B) monopolistic competition because there are many firms in the market
- (C) monopolistic competition because there are no barriers to enter the market
- (D) perfect competition because these products are essentially the same thing
- (E) oligopolistic because so few companies produce these types of products

139. If price is rising to the break-even point as more and more firms exit the market, then

- (A) there is a consumer shortage
- (B) the market structure is a monopolistic competition
- (C) P < ATC in a perfect competition
- (D) P > ATC in a perfect competition
- (E) P = ATC in a perfect competition

140. Which of the following would a monopolist support?

- (A) Output should be MR = MC and P > MC.
- (B) Output should be MR = MC and P = MC.
- (C) Output should be MR > MC and P > MC.
- (D) Output should be MR < MC and P > MC.
- (E) Output should be MR = MC and P < TRC.

141. Which market structures have ease of entry and exit in the long run?

- (A) Perfect competition and monopoly
- (B) Perfect competition and monopolistic competition
- (C) Monopolistic competition and oligopoly
- (D) Oligopoly and natural monopoly
- (E) All market structures have both characteristics.

142. The government is needed to step in and regulate an electric natural monopoly. What must be done to ensure an efficient output is achieved?
    (A) Regulate the natural monopoly to the point where P < MC
    (B) Regulate the natural monopoly to the point where P > MC
    (C) Regulate the natural monopoly to the point where P = MC
    (D) Regulate the natural monopoly to the point where P > TFC
    (E) None of the above

143. Marginal utility refers to
    (A) the change in total utility as a result of the consumption of an additional unit of a good
    (B) the change in a firm's total cost from hiring an additional unit of labor
    (C) the change in saving caused by change in disposable income
    (D) the additional cost of production for one more unit of output
    (E) the additional benefit received from the consumption of the next unit of a good

144. Peter loves french fries, and his friends dared him to eat nothing but french fries all day long. He greatly enjoyed eating 50 french fries, but when he consumed another 50 fries, he enjoyed them less and less because his stomach began to hurt. What does this scenario represent?
    (A) Marginal utility
    (B) Law of diminishing marginal utility
    (C) MC = MB
    (D) MB > MC
    (E) A, B, and D

145. The key difference between accounting profit and economic profit is
    (A) accounting profit includes the opportunity cost of capital
    (B) economic profit includes the opportunity cost of capital
    (C) economic profit is a key component of GDP
    (D) economic profit is usually higher than accounting profit
    (E) accounting profit is always higher than economic profit

146. Cindy left her $75,000-a-year job teaching high school economics to start her own furniture store business. She used $50,000 to start the business. The first year the store took in $150,000 in revenue. What was Cindy's accounting and economic profit?

(A) Accounting profit: $100,000; Economic profit: $25,000
(B) Accounting profit: $100,000; Economic profit: $75,000
(C) Accounting profit: $150,000; Economic profit: $25,000
(D) Accounting profit: $150,000; Economic profit: $50,000
(E) Accounting profit: $100,000; Economic profit: $125,000

147. Allocative inefficiency is a hallmark of which market structure?

(A) Oligopoly
(B) Perfect competition
(C) Natural monopoly
(D) Monopoly
(E) Monopolistic competition

148. An airline may identify a specific group of people and charge them a different rate. This is known as

(A) a monopolistic competition
(B) price discrimination
(C) diseconomies of scale
(D) constant returns to scale
(E) illegal by current federal laws

149. Price discrimination might be successful if

(A) the firm can prevent resale to other consumers and identify and separate groups of consumers
(B) the firm does not have a monopoly on the pricing power of the good or service
(C) the firm has a monopoly on pricing power but cannot prevent resale to other consumers
(D) the firm does not have economies of scale
(E) the firm is operating within government regulations

150. Deirdre is shopping at the mall with her five-year-old daughter. She decides to treat her daughter to a small toy. They browse the aisles of a toy store and come across two dolls. Both dolls are essentially the same in appearance, except Doll B is $5 more than Doll A. Deirdre ends up buying the more expensive doll because her daughter loves the designs on the box it comes in. This scenario illustrates

    (A) the power of a monopolistic competitive firm using advertising
    (B) MC = MB
    (C) price discrimination
    (D) collusive pricing
    (E) all of the above

Use the following graph to answer question 151.

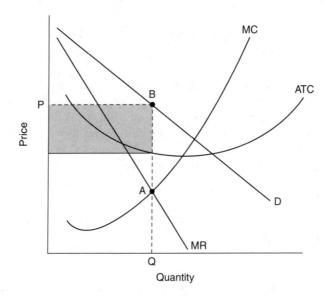

151. The preceding graph represents a short-run monopolistic equilibrium. The shaded area represents

    (A) surplus
    (B) shortage
    (C) profit
    (D) price ceiling
    (E) price floor

152. In the long run, monopolistic competitive firms break even due to

(A) government regulations
(B) price ceilings
(C) entry of new firms into the market
(D) exit of firms from the market
(E) non-price competition

153. Game theory fits best with which market structure?

(A) Monopolistic competition
(B) Perfect competition
(C) Monopoly
(D) Oligopoly
(E) Natural monopoly

154. The government establishes a price ceiling on Good X above the equilibrium price. The result would

(A) raise the price of the good
(B) raise the price of the good and decrease the quantity demanded
(C) lower the price of the good and increase the quantity demanded
(D) lower the price of the good
(E) have no effect on the price of the good or quantity demanded

Use the following graph to answer question 155.

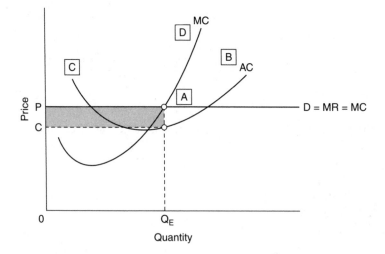

155. Which box represents the profit-maximizing point for a perfectly competitive firm?
    (A) A
    (B) B
    (C) C
    (D) D
    (E) None of the above

156. Which of the following shows the profit-maximizing point for all types of market structures?
    (A) P < MC
    (B) P = MC
    (C) P = ATC
    (D) P = MR
    (E) MR = MC

157. In the market system, resources are allocated in which ways?
    I. Customs and traditions influence which goods and services are produced.
    II. Voluntary exchange influences which goods and services are produced.
    III. Government determines which goods and services are produced.
    (A) I only
    (B) II only
    (C) I and III
    (D) I and II
    (E) I, II, and III

158. Price leadership fits best with which type of market structure?
    (A) Monopoly
    (B) Natural monopoly
    (C) Perfect competition
    (D) Oligopoly
    (E) Monopolistic competition

159. Total variable costs refers to
    (A) costs that do not vary with changes in short-run output
    (B) costs that change with the level of output
    (C) total fixed cost divided by output
    (D) total variable costs divided by output
    (E) none of the above

160. Implicit costs are

(A) direct, purchased, out-of-pocket costs
(B) costs that change with the level of output
(C) indirect costs or opportunity costs
(D) total variable costs divided by output
(E) none of the above

161. All of the following explain the downward slope of the demand curve EXCEPT

(A) income effect
(B) substitution effect
(C) diminishing marginal utility
(D) complement effect
(E) all of the above explain the downward slope of a demand curve

162. If an increase in technology in a perfectly competitive firm only lowers the firm's costs of production, what will the effect be?

	Price	Quantity	Profit
(A)	decrease	decrease	decrease
(B)	decrease	increase	increase
(C)	no change	decrease	increase
(D)	no change	increase	increase
(E)	increase	increase	increase

163. What would be the outcome if an increase in technology lowers a firm's cost of production under a monopoly?

(A) The price will increase.
(B) Consumer surplus will decrease.
(C) The price of the good will decrease.
(D) The price of the good will remain the same.
(E) The price of the good will decrease, and the quantity demanded will increase.

164. Measuring efficiency through allocation of resources is best expressed in which formula?

(A) $P = MC$
(B) $P = AR$
(C) $MB > MC$
(D) $MB = MC$
(E) $P = ATC$

165. For a perfectly competitive firm, what are usually the long-term profits?

    (A) Less than the price equilibrium
    (B) More than the price equilibrium
    (C) Zero
    (D) More than AVC
    (E) Less than TFC and AVC

166. If a cartel comes into existence, the most likely outcome would be that

    (A) economic profits will be balanced among all cartel members
    (B) each cartel member would attempt to cheat by producing more
    (C) there is allocative efficiency
    (D) prices will be established through the market forces of supply and demand
    (E) advertising will push consumers to one firm or the other

167. Monopoly dead weight loss is caused by

    (A) $P > MC$
    (B) $P = MC$
    (C) $MC = MB$
    (D) $MC > MB$
    (E) none of the above

168. If price equals marginal revenue, which equals marginal cost, which equals average total cost, all in the long run, what type of market structure would this be?

    (A) Monopolistic competition
    (B) Monopoly
    (C) Natural monopoly
    (D) Oligopoly
    (E) Perfect competition

169. All of the following are characteristic of an oligopoly EXCEPT

    (A) price taking
    (B) collusive behavior
    (C) barriers to entry
    (D) cheating on other firm members to produce more
    (E) a few large firms

170. Which of the following is a significant factor in monopoly pricing power?

    (A) Barriers to entry
    (B) Advertising
    (C) Price discrimination
    (D) Product differentiation
    (E) All of the above

171. Price elasticity of demand is an extremely useful tool in economics because

    (A) it indicates the equilibrium price
    (B) it predicts the market forces of supply and demand
    (C) it shows how consumer behavior is affected by price
    (D) it predicts how much firms will produce until the shutdown point
    (E) it indicates a balance between long-run and short-run production costs

172. If the government establishes a price less than the market equilibrium price, then it is a

    (A) price floor
    (B) price ceiling
    (C) barrier to entry
    (D) barrier to exit
    (E) none of the above

173. How do economists know that a good is a viable substitute?

    (A) Calculate cross-elasticity and the result is a positive number.
    (B) Calculate cross-elasticity and the result is a negative number.
    (C) The product is price inelastic.
    (D) Wait to see if the market forces of supply and demand balance to equilibrium for the potential substitute.
    (E) None of the above

174. If economic profit is zero, then

    (A) a firm earned a normal profit
    (B) a firm earned an accounting profit
    (C) a firm has reached its shutdown point in the short run
    (D) a firm has reached its shutdown point in the long run
    (E) a firm must lobby the government for assistance in subsidies

175. The freedom of entry and exit for a perfectly competitive market guarantees

(A) each firm knows how each other is planning its production
(B) no cheating on a firm's part to produce an additional unit of output
(C) economic profits will be zero in the long run
(D) economic profits will be greater than accounting profits
(E) economic profits will exceed marginal revenue

176. Producing to where MR = MC in a perfectly competitive market ensures

(A) the government will not intervene with regulations
(B) the ease of entry and exit in the market
(C) product differentiation
(D) earning an economic profit in the long run
(E) production efficiency in the long run

177. If a firm bases its decisions of pricing and production on the actions of other firms, then it is most likely a(n)

(A) monopolistic competition
(B) natural monopoly
(C) monopoly
(D) perfect competition
(E) oligopoly

178. A cartel will maximize profit when

(A) MC = MR
(B) MC < MR
(C) MC > MR
(D) W = MPR
(E) none of the above

179. The significant purpose of a "barrier to entry" in a market is

(A) it helps monopolies earn economic profit
(B) it restricts the creation of a cartel
(C) it restricts price discrimination
(D) it allows monopolistic competitive firms to differentiate their product
(E) it restricts collusive pricing practices

180. The income effect refers to

   (A) the change in the quantity demanded due to a change in price of a relative good
   (B) the change in the quantity demanded due to a change in a consumer's purchasing power
   (C) the change in a consumer's total utility from the consumption of a good
   (D) economic profits will be zero in the long run for a perfectly competitive market
   (E) collusive pricing tactics that oligopolies use

181. Long-run profits for the perfectly competitive firm will always be

   (A) greater than the marginal cost
   (B) normal
   (C) negative
   (D) positive
   (E) none of the above

Use the following graph to answer question 182.

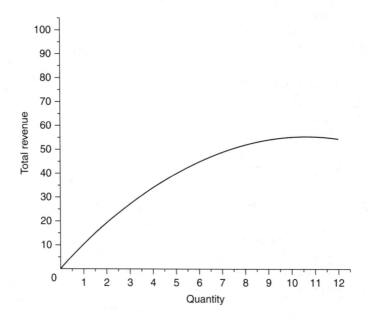

182. The preceding graph represents the
- (A) total cost curve
- (B) total revenue curve
- (C) long-run economic profits for a perfect competitive market
- (D) labor demand
- (E) marginal utility

183. Economies of scale
- (A) are barriers to entry in a monopoly market
- (B) are barriers to exit in a monopoly market
- (C) are an inevitable part of the perfectly competitive market
- (D) are never profitable in the short run
- (E) move directly into diseconomies of scale

184. What occurs when output moves away from P = MC?
- (A) Dead weight loss
- (B) Constant returns to scale
- (C) Diseconomies of scale
- (D) Economies of scale
- (E) A monopoly

185. If P = ATC, then
- (A) economic profit is zero
- (B) accounting profit is zero
- (C) normal profit is unattainable
- (D) firms are operating inefficiently
- (E) all of the above

CHAPTER 3

Factor Markets

186. Derived demand is illustrated by which of the following?

   (A) Consumers desire automobiles to drive, so car companies hire workers for their factories to manufacture automobiles.
   (B) An increase in price increases supply, but demand decreases.
   (C) The price of wheat increases due to inclement weather on crops.
   (D) The salaries of workers increase; thus the price difference is put onto consumers.
   (E) A decrease in the demand for shorts will decrease the demand for flip-flops.

187. To calculate marginal revenue product,

   (A) multiply the marginal product by the marginal cost
   (B) multiply the marginal product by the product price
   (C) divide the marginal product by the marginal cost
   (D) divide the marginal product by the product price
   (E) multiply the marginal revenue by the marginal cost

188. John is starting his own business after years of working as a factory worker. In order to maximize his profit, how many workers should he hire?

   (A) He should hire until the marginal cost equals the marginal revenue.
   (B) He should hire until the marginal product equals wage.
   (C) He should hire until the marginal cost equals wage.
   (D) He should hire until the marginal revenue product equals wage.
   (E) He should hire until the marginal revenue product equals marginal cost.

189. If the automobile industry needed to raise workers' wages, which of the following is a likely result of the labor supply curve?

   (A) The labor supply curve will be horizontal.
   (B) The labor supply curve will be vertical.
   (C) The labor supply curve will shift to the left.
   (D) The labor supply curve will shift to the right.
   (E) There would be no change.

190. How would advancements in technology affect the labor demand curve?

(A) It would be horizontal.
(B) It would be vertical.
(C) It would shift to the right.
(D) It would shift to the left.
(E) There would be no change.

191. If educational advancement courses are offered to employees, how would this affect the productivity of labor?

(A) It would increase.
(B) It would decrease.
(C) It would remain the same.
(D) It would shift the supply curve to the left.
(E) It would have no effect on supply.

192. Beta Industries hires workers for $9 an hour. The price of their product is $5. How many hours of work are required for a marginal revenue product of $40?

(A) 8
(B) 4.5
(C) 20
(D) 36
(E) 50

193. What is the relationship between the MRP curve and the demand curve?

(A) They both slope downward.
(B) They both slope upward.
(C) There is a diminishing marginal return.
(D) They are horizontal in the long run.
(E) They are vertical in the long run.

194. Product demand, productivity, and the availability of technology are examples of

(A) the determinants of supply
(B) the determinants of demand
(C) the determinants of labor demand
(D) the determinants of elasticity of demand
(E) the determinants of labor supply

195. Changes in tastes and immigration reflect

    (A) supply only
    (B) demand only
    (C) product demand
    (D) high elasticity
    (E) reasons why the labor supply curve might shift

196. A single firm that has market power in the labor market is known as a(n)

    (A) purely competitive firm
    (B) monopsony
    (C) oligarchy
    (D) monopolistic competition
    (E) perfect competition

197. Seth finally realized his dream to open a 24-hour bagel café. Which of the following scenarios would increase Seth's demand for labor?

    (A) The price of wheat increases.
    (B) The price of dairy increases.
    (C) The price of wheat decreases.
    (D) A blight destroys thousands of acres of farmland.
    (E) The government establishes a tax on wheat.

198. Derived demand refers to which of the following?

    (A) Labor demand for a business is the MRP curve.
    (B) Demand for labor comes from the demand for the product produced.
    (C) The combination of labor and capital helps minimize total costs.
    (D) A business hires workers to the point where MRP = MRC.
    (E) Certain firms are wage setters.

199. Which of the following is an example of derived demand?

    (A) People desire food to eat, so farms invest in tractors and hire workers.
    (B) The wages of farmhands increase, so supply decreases and demand increases.
    (C) The wages of farmhands decrease, so supply increases and demand decreases.
    (D) People desire food to eat, so farms raise the price of food.
    (E) None of the above

200. All of the following will increase the demand for doctors EXCEPT

(A) there is an increase in government subsidies given to college students studying premed
(B) a philanthropist donates a new research facility wing to a hospital
(C) a cure is found for the common cold
(D) the American Medical Association decreases the credit requirements needed to receive a medical degree
(E) all the above increase demand

201. If the output effect is greater than the substitution effect, what will happen to the demand for labor?

(A) Increases
(B) Decreases
(C) Increases and then gradually decreases
(D) Decreases and then gradually increases
(E) Remains the same

202. An increase in a firm's MRP will result in

(A) a decrease in demand
(B) an increase in demand
(C) a shift of the supply curve to the left
(D) a change in labor demanded
(E) none of the above

203. The marginal revenue product refers to which of the following?

(A) It measures the cost a business must pay for using one more unit of a factor of production.
(B) It is the value that the next unit of a resource brings to the firm.
(C) The combination of labor and capital helps minimize total costs.
(D) A business hires workers to the point where MRP = MRC.
(E) Certain firms are wage setters.

204. If a firm is experiencing wages to be greater than MRP, what is the best course of action?

(A) Hire more workers
(B) Increase supply
(C) Decrease supply
(D) Lay off workers
(E) Do nothing

205. A decrease in the price of machinery will likely have which result?

(A) The demand for labor will increase.
(B) The demand for labor will decrease.
(C) The supply of machinery will decrease.
(D) Firms will hire to the point where MRP = W.
(E) Total revenue will increase.

206. If the price of resources decreases, which of the following is the most likely result?

(A) Labor demand will increase.
(B) Labor demand will decrease.
(C) The supply curve will shift to the left.
(D) The supply curve will become horizontal.
(E) All of the above

207. Immigration has which of the following effects?

(A) It will move the labor supply curve from their country of origin to the right. In the country to which they moved, the curve will shift to the left.
(B) It will move the labor supply curve from their country of origin to the right. In the country to which they moved, the curve will shift to the right.
(C) It will move the labor supply curve from their country of origin to the left. In the country to which they moved, the curve will shift to the right.
(D) It will increase revenue for firms.
(E) It will decrease the labor demand curves.

208. If the factors of production increase, what will happen to labor demand?

(A) Labor demand will increase.
(B) Labor demand will remain the same.
(C) Labor demand will decrease.
(D) Labor demand will drive prices lower.
(E) Labor demand will have no effect on price.

209. What will happen to labor demand if the price of a complementary resource rises?

(A) Labor demand will decrease.
(B) Labor demand will remain the same.
(C) Labor demand will increase.
(D) Labor demand will force the price of the product lower.
(E) Labor demand will have no effect on price.

210. The least-cost hiring rule refers to

(A) firms that are wage setters
(B) a business hiring workers to the point where MRP = MRC
(C) the combination of labor and capital helping minimize total costs
(D) measuring the cost a business must pay for using one more unit of a factor of production
(E) the value that the next unit of a resource brings to the firm

211. How does a monopsony find the equilibrium number of workers to hire?

(A) MRP = W
(B) MRP < W
(C) MRC > W
(D) MC < MB
(E) MC = MB

212. Demand for labor is a

(A) derived demand
(B) product of positive externalities
(C) product of negative externalities
(D) function of product markets
(E) function of the elasticity of demand

213. Where will you find equilibrium in a competitive labor market?

(A) MFC = MRP
(B) MRP = MRC
(C) MRC = W
(D) MRP = W
(E) MC = MB

214. All else equal, as the price of labor increases,

(A) unemployment decreases
(B) employment decreases
(C) the supply of labor remains the same
(D) demand remains the same
(E) none of the above

CHAPTER 4

Market Failure and the Role of Government

215. If a negative externality emerges, what may happen to marginal social cost?

(A) Marginal social cost is put off onto consumers.

(B) The supply curve does not represent marginal social cost.

(C) Government intervention will help establish MSC = MEC.

(D) MSC = MPC

(E) MSC = MPB

216. If a positive externality emerges, what may happen to the demand curve?

(A) MEB is not represented.

(B) MEC is represented.

(C) MSC is represented.

(D) Marginal private benefits are not represented.

(E) None of the above

The following graph represents a government intervention in response to a market that produced a positive externality. Use the information provided in the graph to answer questions 217 and 218.

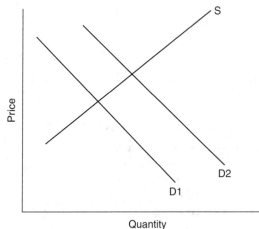

217. How may the government intervene to move the demand curve from D1 to D2?

    (A) Give a subsidy to buyers

    (B) Tax buyers

    (C) Influence the business making the good to stop production

    (D) Increase the money supply

    (E) Decrease the money supply

218. Since the demand curve is now at D2, all of the following are true EXCEPT

    (A) resources are being efficiently used

    (B) MEB is now represented in the demand curve

    (C) output is now at the socially optimum level

    (D) MEB is not represented in the demand curve

    (E) all of the above are true

The following graph represents a government intervention in response to a market that produced a negative externality. Use the information provided in the graph to answer questions 219 and 220.

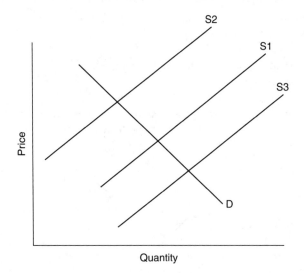

219. Establishing a direct control on producers will

    (A) shift the supply curve from S1 to S2

    (B) shift the supply curve from S2 to S3

    (C) have no effect on the supply curve

    (D) create a new demand curve

    (E) both A and D are correct

220. If the supply curve is shifted to S2, which of the following is TRUE?

(A) Marginal costs are not reflected in the supply curve.

(B) Marginal costs are reflected in the supply curve.

(C) Output has reached the socially optimum level.

(D) The demand curve will also shift to the left.

(E) Both B and C are correct.

221. A private business will not produce a good like a public radio station, because

(A) MC is greater than MB

(B) there is zero profit for this good

(C) the government owns a monopoly for this type of service

(D) the free-rider problem

(E) all of the above

222. The idea that taxes and a person's income should vary directly is known as

(A) the marginal propensity to consume

(B) the marginal propensity to save

(C) the free-rider problem

(D) the ability to pay principle of taxation

(E) marginal cost

223. The reason a general sales tax is regressive is because

(A) low-income families pay a higher portion of their income than high-income families do

(B) the tax is paid for by the seller, not the buyer

(C) the tax is paid for by the buyer, not the seller

(D) low-income families pay less of the tax than households with higher income do

(E) tax rates do not vary as compared to income

224. The fact that a firefighter's job is more dangerous than a college professor's job is an example of

(A) compensating differential

(B) a negative externality

(C) the free-rider problem

(D) the ability to pay principle

(E) the benefits received principle

225. All of the following are examples of compensating differential EXCEPT

    (A) a teaching assistant earning less than a sanitation worker

    (B) a worker with 15 years' experience making more than a worker with 2 years' experience in the same field

    (C) an airline pilot earning less than a neurologist

    (D) a principal earning more than a substitute teacher

    (E) A and B are viable examples

226. Of the following, which is a public good?

    (A) a limousine

    (B) tickets to a baseball game

    (C) a subscription to the *New York Times*

    (D) a radio station

    (E) a bowl of ice cream

227. A "flat tax" is also known as

    (A) ability to pay tax

    (B) benefits received tax

    (C) proportional tax

    (D) income tax

    (E) property tax

228. Industrialized nations often produce negative externalities in the form of pollution. What is a possible solution to fix this negative externality?

    (A) A tax on consumers

    (B) A government subsidy for consumers

    (C) A government subsidy for producers

    (D) A tax on producers

    (E) A flat tax on both producers and consumers

229. Last year Anna earned $50,000 in gross income and paid $10,000 in taxes. She recently received a promotion. So next year she will earn $75,000 in gross income and pay $15,000 in taxes. This increase in taxes is a result of

    (A) a regressive tax

    (B) a progressive tax

    (C) a proportional tax

    (D) an ability to pay tax

    (E) none of the above

230. The fire department is an example of a(n)

   (A) private good
   (B) inferior good
   (C) normal good
   (D) public good
   (E) complementary good

231. Nation A has a high Gini ratio. You can conclude that Nation A

   (A) has a highly unequal distribution of income
   (B) has a more equal distribution of income
   (C) has no unequal distribution of income
   (D) is allocating its resources in full efficiency
   (E) is at full employment and no inflation

Use the following diagram to answer questions 232 and 233.

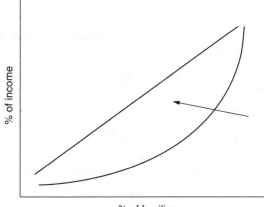

232. The preceding diagram represents

   (A) the percentage of income tax families pay in the United States
   (B) the percentage of families paying a regressive tax on their incomes
   (C) the percentage of families paying a flat tax on their incomes
   (D) the percentage of families paying a progressive tax in the United States
   (E) the distribution of income among families in the United States

233. The arrow in the preceding diagram is pointing to the area between a perfect distribution of income and the actual distribution of income. If the Gini ratio is 0.9, it is said that this diagram represents

(A) a highly unequal distribution of income
(B) a very equal distribution of income
(C) most families having the same socioeconomic status
(D) a society benefiting from egalitarianism
(E) a negative externality

234. Suppose Anna earns $50,000 a year and pays $10,000 in taxes. Her friend Sarah earns $100,000 a year and pays only $12,000 a year in taxes. This is an example of

(A) a progressive tax
(B) a proportional tax
(C) a negative externality
(D) being in a higher tax bracket
(E) a regressive tax

235. Market power, a person's ability, human capital, and discrimination are all factors that may result in

(A) an unequal distribution of wealth
(B) negative externalities
(C) positive externalities
(D) a low Gini ratio
(E) a fair and equal distribution of wealth

236. If income increases and the average tax rate falls, this is also known as a

(A) regressive tax
(B) proportional tax
(C) flat tax
(D) progressive tax
(E) tax bracket

237. As income increases, the average tax rate increases. This is known as a

(A) progressive tax
(B) regressive tax
(C) flat tax
(D) proportional tax
(E) tax bracket

238. A ride in a taxicab is a form of

(A) a public good
(B) a private good
(C) a government subsidy
(D) a positive externality
(E) the free-rider problem

239. NASA sends a satellite into space and receives a transmission from an alien world. The next day all the newspaper headlines read, "We Are Not Alone in the Universe!" Brian, the economist, reads the article and realizes that the satellite is a form of

(A) a private good
(B) a government subsidy
(C) a positive externality
(D) a public good
(E) the free-rider problem

240. The government helps with the redistribution of income

(A) only in a command economy
(B) only in a mixed economy
(C) through taxes
(D) through proportional taxes only
(E) through government subsidies and education training

241. Christopher recently moved out of his parent's house and purchased his own house. He worked all summer on the front- and backyard lawns and gardens to make his new house look nice. Christopher's new neighbors all appreciated the hard work he put into the outside of his house, as it helped beautify their block and neighborhood. The results of Christopher's efforts are known as

(A) the free-rider problem
(B) positive externalities
(C) the spillover effect
(D) the Gini ratio
(E) negative externalities

242. A good that is excludable to other consumers is known as a

    (A) public good
    (B) negative externality
    (C) positive externality
    (D) government subsidy
    (E) private good

243. A good that is nonexcludable to other consumers is known as a

    (A) public good
    (B) negative externality
    (C) positive externality
    (D) government subsidy
    (E) private good

244. If the U.S. government increases a tax to help redistribute income from the wealthy to the poor, it is following a

    (A) proportional tax system
    (B) tariff system
    (C) progressive tax system
    (D) regressive tax system
    (E) neutral tax system

245. A negative externality will exist when

    (A) all consumers receive an equal share of economic resources
    (B) spillover costs are given to others not directly involved in the consumption or production of a good or service
    (C) the production of a good or service creates a spillover benefit
    (D) when members of a community pay for a good or service while others do not yet benefit
    (E) there is a large unequal distribution of income in a society

246. The private sector will not provide for a public good or service due to

    (A) the income effect
    (B) the interest-rates effect
    (C) the free-rider problem
    (D) spillover costs
    (E) all of the above

247. A positive externality will exist when
   (A) all consumers receive an equal share of economic resources
   (B) spillover costs are given to others not directly involved in the consumption or production of a good or service
   (C) the production of a good or service creates a spillover benefit
   (D) when members of a community pay for a good or service while others do not yet benefit
   (E) there is an equal distribution of income in a society

248. If producers of a good or service overallocate their resources, then
   (A) a negative externality exists
   (B) a positive externality exists
   (C) spillover costs are subsidized by the government
   (D) the firm is at the shutdown point
   (E) A, C, and D

249. Which of the following illustrate a public good?
   I. Firefighters
   II. Traffic lights
   III. A bean burrito
   IV. Attending a private school
   (A) I only
   (B) I and II
   (C) I, II, and III
   (D) II and IV
   (E) I, II, and IV

250. Regulation and antitrust laws
   (A) are some of the economic functions of the government that help encourage competition
   (B) some of the economic functions of the government that dissuade competition
   (C) are effective only in a market economy
   (D) assist the government to redistribute income and wealth
   (E) are methods used by the government to promote positive externalities

ANSWERS

Chapter 1: Basic Economic Concepts

1. (C) Choice C is the best answer because the resources in the world are limited, yet our desires and wants are unlimited. The study of economics attempts to examine the ways these unlimited wants and desire may be satisfied.

2. (D) Deirdre can make only one decision regarding how she will spend her time. An opportunity cost represents the next best thing missed out on. In this case, it is missing out on the $10/hour babysitting job and not the $7/hour library job. All other choices are incorrect because they incorporate the two choices, whereas opportunity costs represent only the next best alternative.

3. (A) With any choice people make, they must look at the relationship between marginal benefit and marginal cost. If a decision, whether it be purchasing an item or going for a walk, costs more than the benefit, then the person should not do it.

4. (E) The production possibilities curve represents the maximum output between two goods. It also reflects the opportunity costs between these two goods because resources are scarce. Any point along the curve is the maximum output producing both of the goods, and therefore is an attainable and efficient use of resources. Economic growth is represented by a rightward shift of the production possibilities curve. Choice E is the best answer because Point E represents an attainable and efficient use of resources and Point B represents a point of economic growth.

5. (A) The production possibilities curve represents the maximum output between two goods using scarce resources. As such, it represents the opportunity costs incurred when the production shifts to more of one product than the other. The more a producer chooses to make of a product, the more the opportunity cost increases for the product not being produced. This represents the law of increasing costs.

6. (E) Trade will exist between two countries if there is a comparative advantage between the two countries, or each country is producing its good at a lower opportunity cost than the other.

7. (D) If a society is overallocating, then it is not utilizing its resources to efficiency. This would imply that the marginal benefit (MB) for producing goods and services with these resources is less than the marginal cost (MC). In any economic decision, it is best to have either MB > MC or MB = MC.

8. (C) Choice C is the best answer because it best reflects the idea of comparative advantage. If a producer can make a good at a lower opportunity cost than all other producers, it is said that he or she has a comparative advantage. Richard can mow the lawn at a lower opportunity cost than Michele, so it would be mutually beneficial if he mowed the lawn and Michele walked the dog.

9. (C) A command economy is the opposite of a free market (where prices and the answers to the fundamental questions of economics are answered by consumers and producers). A command economy is also known as a planned economy.

10. (A) The production possibilities curve represents the maximum production capabilities of two goods based on an economy's available resources. An outward, or rightward, shift of the production possibilities curve represents economic growth. Choice A is the best answer because educational training would be an increase in human capital and in production. All the other choices would cause the production possibilities curve to shift to the left.

11. (C) The production possibilities curve represents the maximum output between two goods using scarce resources. Any point lying on the curve would represent the most attainable, efficient use of resources in production.

12. (E) The number of resources in the world is limited, yet our desires and wants are unlimited. For example, there is only a finite amount of fossil fuels available in the earth.

13. (E) Specialization refers to the production of goods based on comparative advantage. If a nation can produce a good at a lower opportunity cost, then it would be beneficial if it specialized in producing that good and traded with another nation that specialized in producing other goods.

14. (A) Factors of production refer to all the units that are used in the production of goods and services in hopes of making a profit. They are categorized as land, labor, capital, and entrepreneurship.

15. (B) The law of increasing costs refers to how the more a good or service is produced, the more its opportunity costs increase. If there is an increase in the production of Good A, then the opportunity cost, the next most valuable alternative, increases for Good B.

16. (A) If the production possibilities curve is a straight line, then where resource materials are best suited for the production of both goods, either opportunity costs are constant or resources are not specialized.

17. (A) Trade will exist between two countries if there is a comparative advantage between the two countries, or each country is producing its good at a lower opportunity cost than the other.

18. (B) Specialization refers to the production of goods based on comparative advantage. If a nation can produce a good at a lower opportunity cost, then it would be beneficial if it specialized in producing that good and traded with another nation that specialized in producing other goods. Obtaining more than the production possibilities curve dictates necessitates specialization.

19. (A) According to the law of comparative advantage, two nations should specialize production by producing goods at the lowest possible cost. These nations should then engage in trade for the products they stopped producing to specialize. Since Spain has a lower opportunity cost for producing soccer balls as compared to Germany, it should stop producing golf balls and focus on soccer balls.

20. (A) Choice A is the best answer because a free market guides producers to the three fundamental questions: What to produce? How to produce? How much to produce? All businesses must decide what to produce based on limited resources (scarcity). Entrepreneurs must answer the question "How to produce?" because it affects major businesses decisions: Should the product be produced domestically or abroad? Should outside contractors be consulted? In a free market, the question of how much to produce is dictated by supply and demand, where prices and output inform producers on production levels for optimization.

21. (D) Economic growth occurs if any of the factors of production increase. Any choice that refers to a decrease in the factors of production may be eliminated. Choice B is incorrect because although a division of labor is highly efficient, it is ambiguous if it would create economic growth. A diseconomy of scale refers to an increase in cost when output is increased.

22. (B) With any choice people make, they must look at the relationship between marginal benefit and marginal cost. If a decision, whether it be purchasing an item or going for a walk, costs more than the benefit, then the person should not do it.

23. (C) Opportunity cost is what is given up when someone makes a decision. If your school decides to construct a new performing arts center, all of the resources that could have been used in another project are given up. The resources must go into the construction of the performing arts center.

24. (E) Allocative efficiency refers to the measure of the benefit or utility gained from the use of material resources. If resources are being used efficiently, then the production possibilities curve will remain the same and production will lie on the line, not inside. All other choices would result in a shift of the production possibilities curve because these would be changes in the factors of production.

25. (D) Marginal analysis refers to the decision-making process based on marginal benefits versus marginal costs.

26. (B) Choice B is the best answer because a market system is characterized by a decentralization of decision making for firms and consumers. A mixed economy refers to a combination of capitalism and socialism, where there are elements of centralized planning and a free market. A command economy is the opposite of a free market (where prices and the answers to the fundamental questions of economics are answered by consumers and producers). A command economy is also known as a planned economy.

27. (C) When comparing command economies, mixed economies, or a market economy, the most fundamental differences exist in how these societies answer the three fundamental questions of economics: What to produce? How to produce? How much to produce?

28. (D) This refers to the three fundamental questions of economics: What to produce? How to produce? How much to produce? These questions exist because resources are scarce and people's wants and desires are unlimited.

29. (A) Microeconomics analyzes the market behavior of individual firms and consumers. Choices B, C, and D are microeconomic variables because they focus on the small-scale economic decisions of firms and consumers. Choice A is a macroeconomic variable because it focuses on a large-scale, nationwide element of unemployment.

30. (D) A market system is characterized by a decentralization of decision making for firms and consumers.

Chapter 2: The Nature and Function of Product Markets

31. (A) According to the law of demand, all else being equal, when the price of a good or service increases, the quantity demanded decreases. Choice A is the best answer because it is the inverse of the question being asked.

32. (B) A normal good is a good that increases in demand as income increases. Since Michael received an increase in his yearly salary, there was an increase in demand for steak, and steak is an expensive meat product, it is a normal good. Choice A is incorrect because an inferior good is a good for which demand decreases as income increases. Choice E is incorrect because eating steak is not a necessity. Choices C and D are incorrect because eating steak does not affect the determinants of supply and demand.

33. (D) An inferior good is a good for which demand decreases as income increases. Since Peter received an increase in salary, he can afford better shoes than thrift-store-bought shoes.

34. (E) Tin is a factor of production used in the production of guitar strings. Firms will produce more guitar strings if the costs related to the production of the product decrease. If the price of tin decreases, then producers are willing and able to produce more due to a decrease in a factor of production.

35. (C) Remember that people will buy more of a good if the price is low and less of a good if the price is high. This illustrates an inverse relationship. According to the law of demand and all else being equal, when the price of a good or service increases, the quantity demanded decreases.

36. (B) The law of supply represents the willingness of producers to produce goods at all price levels. The law of supply shows a direct relationship between price and quantity of goods supplied. Therefore, if the price of a good increases, producers are more willing to produce an increased quantity of goods.

37. (A) Within a market system, consumers and firms are free to consume and produce what they wish. The three fundamental questions asked in an economy are, What to produce? How to produce? How much to produce? These questions are answered by the decisions made by consumers and producers, where prices are set through the market forces of supply and demand without any government intervention.

38. (B) The question asks for only the quantity supplied, so any question that refers to price may be eliminated. Choice B is the best answer because if the price of a good increases, its substitutes will experience an increase in the quantity demanded.

39. (C) Competition ensures that prices will be controlled through the market forces of supply and demand. If a monopoly exists, that firm may set a much higher price than in a perfectly competitive market. If competition exists, then it will increase the total welfare and benefit society.

40. (E) Tennis rackets and tennis balls are complementary goods. You cannot use a tennis racket without tennis balls. Therefore, if the price of one good increases or decreases, the price of the complementary good increases or decreases. Choice E is the best answer because it illustrates the complementary effect.

41. (A) Chicken is a normal good. Remember that a normal good is a good that increases in demand as income increases. If the demand curve for chicken shifted to the left, then consumer income would show an overall decrease.

42. (A) An indifference curve illustrates the levels of utility or satisfaction for a consumer when he or she is presented with a combination of goods. If the consumer is indifferent between Variety of Goods A and Variety of Goods B, then the consumer will receive the same level of satisfaction between the varieties of goods. This curve is used in the study of consumer choice and represents how consumers are faced with trade-offs and restraints on their budgets. Remember that consumers have unlimited wants but face limited resources.

43. (C) Hot dogs and hot dog buns are complementary goods. If the price of hot dogs increases, then the price of hot dog buns will increase as well.

44. (B) All else being equal, in a free market system, the price of a good or service is determined at the equilibrium point where supply and demand intersect.

45. (A) The graph represents the inverse relation stated in the law of demand. The graph represents movement from Point B to Point A. This illustrates that the quantity demanded decreased due to an increase in price.

46. (C) If the price of a key ingredient decreases, then the cost of production will decrease. This will lead Doherty Industries to offer more of the product at all possible price levels. This illustrates the law of supply.

47. (E) Elasticity refers to the measure of sensitivity of the price of a good or service if there is a change in price. If a product is inelastic, then it is said to not vary in demand if there is a change in price. For example, gasoline is price inelastic because a change in price does not change the demand; people still need to fill up their gas tanks. If a producer produces a good that is price inelastic and wished to increase total revenue, then he or she would simply have to raise the price.

48. (A) Refer to question 47. Most necessity goods are price inelastic.

49. (B) The elasticity formula is percent change in quantity divided by percent change in price. If the answer is greater than 1, the good is said to be price sensitive, or elastic. If the answer is less than 1, the good is said not to be price sensitive. Therefore, Choice B is the best answer because 40/10 = 4.

50. (D) Refer to question 49. Therefore, Choice D is the best answer because 0/30 = 0.

51. (E) Choice E is the best answer because all other choices influence demand, whereas the percent change in the quantity demanded is part of the formula for elasticity.

52. (B) The movement from D1 to D2 represents an increase in demand. Choice B is the best answer because a decrease in the price of a substitute good would decrease demand for this product and increase demand for the substitute good.

53. (A) The movement from S1 to S2 represents a decrease in supply. Choice A is the best answer because if the price of a key ingredient to the production of the product decreased, then production would increase due to a decrease in the costs of production.

54. (D) A price ceiling refers to the maximum price at which a producer is allowed to sell a good or service. This is usually instituted by law from the government and helps ensure fair business practices. A price ceiling is set by observing the point below the equilibrium price.

55. (A) Choice A is the best answer because over a longer period of time, producers have a better chance to adjust to a change in price: hire more workers and build more plants. Over time, elasticity of supply will be greater.

56. (C) Consumer surplus is measured by the calculating the difference between what consumers are willing and able to pay for a good or service and its relative market price. A surplus occurs if the consumer is willing to pay more than the market price for a good or service.

57. (A) If there is a change in price, then there would be movement only on the demand curve and not a shift of the demand curve to the left or right. Choice A is the best answer because a change in the price of golf clubs would be reflected as movement along the demand curve. All other choices would illustrate a change in demand.

58. (A) An increase in demand will signal to suppliers to raise the prices of their products. If demand rises, then suppliers will raise their prices and a higher quantity will be sold.

59. (C) Since there was an increase in price for Product X, a decrease in demand should result. If the demand for Product Z increases as a result of an increase in the price of Product X, then Product Z is a substitute good.

60. (B) A price ceiling refers to the maximum price at which a producer is allowed to sell a good or service. This is usually instituted by law from the government and helps to ensure fair business practices. If credit card companies are regulated to institute a maximum amount on how much interest they can charge, then it is a price ceiling.

61. (B) A shortage is defined as a situation where the quantity demanded exceeds the quantity supplied. More and more people are demanding a particular good, but producers do not have an adequate supply of the good.

62. (A) Choice A is the best answer because it reflects the law of supply: producers are more willing and able to produce more of a good as price increases.

63. (A) Choice A is the best answer because the invisible hand is a reference to the ideas of economist Adam Smith in 1776. If producers act in their own self-interest, then society as a whole will benefit through trade and entrepreneurship. No government intervention is needed; the economy will correct itself in the long run.

64. (D) The determinants of supply refer to the external factors that influence supply. If these determinants change, then the supply curve will shift to the left or the right. Some of the determinants of supply are price, available technology, the number of producers in the market, and taxes imposed by the government.

65. (D) A surplus exists when the quantity supplied is greater than the quantity demanded. A surplus is another way of saying there is an excess of supply. Choice B is incorrect because the equilibrium point is the intersection between supply and demand, where the supply equals the demand. Choice C is incorrect because it refers to the percentage of income distribution in a society.

66. (A) A price floor refers to a legal minimum price below which the product cannot be sold. If a surplus exists, then an effective price floor would help remove the surplus due to the decrease in price and subsequent increased demand.

67. (A) Economies of scale refers to the downward part of the long-run average total cost (LRAC) curve where LRAC falls as plant size rises; constant returns to scale refers to changes in output by the same proportion as a change in input; and diseconomies of scale refers to the upward sloping part of the LRAC where firms see an increase in marginal cost as output increases. Choice A is the best answer because it reflects these definitions.

68. (C) Choice C is the best answer because if there are too few substitutes and little time for changes to production to be made, then demand is said to be inelastic. Therefore, substitutes and time are determinants of elasticity.

69. (A) Since there are too few substitutes for cigarettes, then demand would be inelastic for cigarettes.

70. (A) The elasticity formula is percent change in quantity divided by percent change in price. If the answer is greater than 1, the good is said to be price sensitive. If the answer is less than 1, the good is said not to be price sensitive. Therefore, $4/2 = 2$ and would be price elastic.

71. (B) A surplus refers to when the quantity supplied is greater than the quantity demanded. It is graphically represented above the equilibrium point. Choice A is incorrect because it refers to a price ceiling. Choice C is incorrect because it refers to diseconomies of scale.

72. (A) Dead weight loss refers to the lost net benefit to society caused by a movement from competitive market equilibrium. In other words, the people who would purchase the good and have more marginal benefit (MB) than marginal price are not purchasing the product. Therefore, MC > MB, and dead weight loss occurs.

73. (A) Dead weight loss refers to the lost net benefit to society caused by a movement from competitive market equilibrium. In other words, the people who would purchase the good and have more marginal benefit (MB) than marginal price are not purchasing the product. Therefore, MC > MB, and dead weight loss occurs.

74. (A) The law of diminishing marginal utility states that as a person increases consumption of a good, satisfaction or utility decreases with each marginal consumption of the good. For example, say you really liked hot dogs and you started eating them every day. With consumption of each hot dog, there would come a point where you would like them less and less.

75. (C) The elasticity formula is percent change in quantity divided by percent change in price. If the answer is greater than 1, the good is said to be price sensitive. If the answer is less than 1, the good is said not to be price sensitive. However, if the answer is zero, then the demand is completely independent from the price. Consumers will purchase the good regardless of the price.

76. (E) Sole proprietorships are the largest business type in the United States. However, they are the smallest in terms of total revenue. A sole proprietorship runs the risk of liability if the business fails and the owner cannot cover costs and repay loans. The bank may take the owner's assets if this occurs. This is unlike a corporation, where business owners are protected with limited liability: responsibility does not go further than the amount originally invested in the business.

77. (A) The principal-agent problem refers to the conflicts of interest that arise between a principal and an agent over the hazards of a job to be performed. While it may be of a huge benefit to the principal, it comes at a greater cost to the agent. This problem is a part of game theory. Choice B is incorrect because it refers to those individuals who benefit from a product without incurring any of the costs.

78. (E) Limited liability refers to the notion that what a person is liable for in a business investment does not exceed the amount of the original investment. If you start a business with limited liability but go bankrupt, then you would not lose your personal assets. It is beneficial for all types of businesses.

79. (A) If a business owns plants at various stages of production, then it is a vertically integrated firm. This means that a business expands to different points along the same production path.

80. (A) Choice A is the best answer because spillover costs refer to the additional costs to a society and not to part of the supply curve from the production of a good. The government would intervene either in the form of a tax on producers to limit production or to internalize the spillover cost into the supply curve.

81. (E) The firm is a business organization that utilizes the factors of production to produce a good or service.

82. (B) A monopoly is a market structure where one firm is the producer for a good or service with very few substitutes and many barriers to entry. Therefore, a monopoly may set a very high price for its product. The role of the government is to intervene and break up monopolies, fostering competition.

83. (B) A monopolistic competition refers to a market structure with a few firms producing a differentiated product with easy entry into the market. Choice A is the wrong answer because it refers to a natural monopoly. Choice C is incorrect because it refers to an oligopoly. Choice D is incorrect because it refers to a perfect competition. Choice E is incorrect because it refers to a monopoly.

84. (C) An oligopoly is a market structure where there are a small number of interdependent firms producing either a standardized or differentiated product with barriers to entry. Choice A is incorrect because it refers to a natural monopoly. Choice B is incorrect because it refers to a monopoly. Choice D is incorrect because it refers to a monopolistic competition. Choice E is incorrect because it refers to a perfect competition.

85. (A) A monopoly is a market structure where one firm is the producer for a good or service with very few substitutes and many barriers to entry. There is virtually no competition in a monopoly market structure.

86. (A) A perfect competition is a market structure where many firms are producing very similar products, prices are established through supply and demand, and there is freedom to enter and exit the market.

87. (A) In a monopolistic competition, product differentiation is utilized to make a product stand out from its competitors. For example, there are many similarities between the iPhones and BlackBerry smartphones, but there are very subtle differences that appeal to different consumers. In a monopoly, there are very few substitutes for the product.

88. (E) Choice E is the best answer because a perfect competition is a market structure where many firms are producing very similar products, prices are established through supply and demand, and there is freedom to enter and exit the market.

89. (D) A natural monopoly is a market structure where it is beneficial for one firm to control the production of a good or service. For example, natural gas and the water authority work most efficiently and with the greatest benefit if there is a natural monopoly. It would be too complicated and at a great cost if competitive markets began running separate lines to households for gas and water.

90. (B) Choice B is the best answer because the diagram illustrates price equal to marginal revenue. This is true in a perfect competition.

91. (A) Choice A is the best answer because at any other level the firm runs the possibility of producing too much or too little, which would raise revenue or incur a cost.

92. (C) The goal of any firm is to make a profit with the products it is producing and selling. In a perfectly competitive market, there are no barriers to entry into the market. When a product is profitable for a perfectly competitive firm, it exists only in the short run. In the long run, profits are zero because of other firms entering the market.

93. (D) Even though Company Z does not own all the farmland used in the production of tobacco, it owns a significant majority. It now controls most of the farmland used in the production of tobacco. This shows that Company Z is attempting to establish a monopoly by controlling one of the factors of production (land). Choice C is incorrect because even though it is correct that the profit-maximizing point is where MR = MC, it does not relate to the scenario in the question. Choice A is incorrect because all businesses wish to increase profits, and it does not fully answer the question. Choice B is incorrect because an oligopoly refers to a small number of very large firms; this question refers only to Company Z.

94. (C) Market power refers to the ability of a firm to set prices above the perfectly competitive level. A perfectly competitive firm does not have market power, because prices are determined through supply and demand; therefore, a perfect competition is a price taker. A monopoly market structure fits perfectly with the idea of market power because as the only producer of the good, it increases prices above where MR = MC.

95. (A) A monopolistic competition does not have many competitors. Unlike a monopoly, where there is only one firm producing a good, a monopolistic competition has other firms offering slightly different products at different prices. Since the number of competitors is low, a monopolistic firm may increase the price above MR = MC. Choice B is incorrect because a large number of competitors is a characteristic of a perfect competition. Choice C is incorrect because the government encourages patents to help producers earn back what was spent in research and development. Choice D is incorrect because advertising is a tool used in a monopolistic competition to help differentiate their product with a competitor's product but does not give them permission to set any price they wish. Even monopolies and monopolistic competition firms have to pay attention to the law of demand: no consumer will spend $2,000 on a pair of sneakers.

96. (D) In any market structure, the profit-maximizing point is where marginal revenue equals marginal cost. In a perfectly competitive market, price will equal marginal revenue. Choice A is incorrect, although deceiving, because only in the long run will a perfect competition have a zero profit. This is because more and more firms enter the market, cutting price and profit. Choice B is incorrect because the question shows that the firm is profit maximizing and would result in more firms entering, not leaving, the market. Choice C is incorrect because this is a business tactic of an oligopoly.

97. (A) In any market structure the profit-maximizing point is where marginal revenue equals marginal cost. Choice B is incorrect because if the revenue product of labor (MRP) is less than the wages paid to workers, then the firm will respond by laying off workers. Choice C is incorrect because average fixed costs are costs that must be paid regardless if the firm is making a profit or losing money. Choice D is incorrect because economic decisions are not followed through if the marginal cost is greater than the marginal benefit.

98. (A) A patent is a grant given by the government allowing the patent holder the sole right to produce and sell a product for a set period of time. If a producer is the only producer of a product, then it is a monopoly.

99. (A) Economies of scale refers to an increase in the efficiency of a production as production levels increase. Very large economies of scale gives larger companies greater access to a larger market, allowing for the potential for monopolies to be created.

100. (B) Economies of scale refers to an increase in the efficiency of a production as production levels increase. Choice A is incorrect because it describes diseconomies of scale. Choice C is incorrect because if production decreases does not necessarily mean efficiency will increase. Choice D is incorrect because it describes the profit-maximizing point and is unrelated to economies of scale in the short run. Choice E is incorrect because it refers to elasticity.

101. (C) In a monopolistic competition, product differentiation is utilized to make a product stand out from its competitors. For example, there are many similarities between the iPhones and BlackBerry smartphones, but there are very subtle differences that appeal to different consumers.

102. (A) In a monopolistic competition, product differentiation is utilized to make a product stand out from its competitors. There are not as many competitors in a monopolistic competition as compared to a perfect competition, where there are many. As a result, the monopolistic competitive firm must differentiate its product to increase consumer demand. An Italian restaurant is an example of a monopolistic competition. Your neighborhood may have more than one Italian restaurant, but one may have that "secret ingredient" in their sauce that you just love, or other dishes that the other restaurants do not offer. Such a business differentiates its product so that it can stand out from other competitors.

103. (B) Choice B is the best answer because the size of a plant takes time and resources and is not readily available in the short run. All other choices reflect options that may be taken during the short run.

104. (A) The law of diminishing returns states that as more and more units are added to production, there is a point where the marginal revenue product declines. In the short run, marginal cost is low, but as more and more is produced, marginal cost increases.

105. (C) Choices A, B, and D are all variable production units because they can easily be influenced and changed in the short run. However, Choice C is the best answer because human capital refers to the skills and education a worker brings to the production of a product. This is not as easily manipulated by producers in a firm.

106. (C) This question is very straightforward. If a variable production unit—a unit that is not a part of fixed costs—increases, then the marginal cost will increase as well. For example, suppose a plant adds a new machine that uses more electricity than the other machines in the plant. This is an increase in the factors of production, and the firm will respond by increasing the price of the product to cover the additional cost in electricity.

107. (A) Choice A is the best answer because the government ensures that businesses, especially monopolistic competitors, set their prices fairly. The average cost pricing rule states that a business must set a price to its product that is either equal or very close to the costs incurred to produce the good or service. Choice B is incorrect because it refers to the amount of taxes people should pay based on their income levels and ability to pay them. Choice C is incorrect because an antitrust law breaks up a monopoly. Choice D is incorrect because the law of diminishing marginal returns states that as more and more units are added to production, there is a point where the marginal product declines. Choice E is incorrect because economies of scale refers to an increase in the efficiency of a production as production levels increase.

108. (A) Changing the size of the plant is a long-run economic decision. All other choices represent illogical conclusions or are effective only in the long run.

109. (A) Economic profit is the difference between total revenue and total economic cost. Economic profit incorporates opportunity costs, whereas accounting profit does not.

110. (D) Diseconomies of scale exist on the upward sloping part of the LRAC curve. In the long run, firms see increasing costs as production increases.

111. (E) Constant return to scale refers to changes in output by the same proportion as a change in input. It is the point between economies of scale and diseconomies of scale. Choice E is the best answer.

112. (B) Economies of scale refers to an increase in the efficiency of a production as production levels increase. Choice A is incorrect because specialization usually does not result in a decrease in profits. Choice C is incorrect because specialization coincides with a decrease in production costs. Choice D is incorrect because both changes in input are the same as a change in output, so it tends to be a straight line on the LRAC curve. Choice E is incorrect because diseconomies of scale refers to an increase in marginal cost when production increases.

113. (C) Choices A, B, D, and E do employ firms to produce their goods and services, but Choice C offers the definition of a firm, which is what the question is asking.

114. (A) This diagram represents a total cost curve. You should know the differences between the total cost curve and the average total cost curve. This is a total cost curve because of its shape: the curve intercepts the Y-axis positively, which indicates fixed costs; and the rest of the curve illustrates fixed costs plus variable costs.

115. (A) In general, economists say that firms do not go out of business in the short run. They must pay their fixed costs. However, firms may shut down and not pay their variable costs. If Mr. Ray is considering shutting down his business, then the two most important factors he should analyze are average variable cost (AVC) and marginal revenue (MR). The firm will stay open if MR = AVC or MR > AVC. If marginal revenue, the same as price, is equal to average variable costs, then firms could shut down and pay only their fixed costs. If MR < AVC, then firms may shut down.

116. (D) Choice D is the best answer because patents exist as a barrier to entry in a monopoly. A monopolistic competition does not have patents, due to product differentiation.

117. (B) At the point where price is greater than average total costs, more firms will enter the market due to the attractiveness of the business venture. This is so because both fixed and variable costs are being covered by the price. As a result, prices will go down as more and more firms enter the market. Remember, in a perfectly competitive market, economic profit in the long run is zero.

118. (C) Price discrimination refers to a systematic pricing system that charges a different price to different groups of people. However, the firm will still ensure that the maximum price that these different people are willing to pay is utilized. Since the museum is offering a different price to Michele and Richard has to pay full price, it is a form of price discrimination. Another example is a senior citizen discount.

119. (E) Remember that dead weight loss is the lost net benefit to society caused by a movement from competitive market equilibrium. In other words, the people who would purchase the good and have more marginal benefit than marginal price are not purchasing the product. Only in a perfectly competitive market, where price is maintained through supply and demand, will dead weight loss not occur.

120. (E) If an owner of a firm is trying to decide whether to shut down, then analyzing marginal revenue (MR) and average variable cost (AVC) will help. The firm will stay open if MR = AVC or MR > AVC. If marginal revenue, the same as price, is equal to average variable costs, then firms could shut down and pay only their fixed costs. If MR < AVC, then firms may shut down.

121. (A) In any competitive market, the profit-maximizing point is where MR = MC. If MR is greater than MC, then the firm would make a profit. If MC is greater than MR, then the firm would be losing money.

122. (D) A perfectly competitive firm in the long run shows a profit of zero and more and more firms enter the market. Choice D is the best choice because as more and more firms enter the market, and existing markets adjust their size, the price will decrease and all firms will only be making a normal profit.

123. (C) Choice C is the best answer because as more and more firms enter the market, firms react by lowering their capital stock. This will result in causing their marginal cost to decrease.

124. (C) Collusive pricing refers to rival firms all agreeing to disrupt the market equilibrium price of their product. This often occurs in an oligopoly. For example, the firms may all agree to alter the supply of the product to raise prices on the market. Choice C is the best answer because this is an often-used business tactic for cartels.

125. (C) Choice C is the best answer because an oligopoly is a market structure where there are a small number of interdependent firms producing either a standardized or differentiated product with barriers to entry. Very often, the firms may all agree to alter the supply of the product to raise prices on the market.

126. (D) If the price of a good increases, consumers lose purchasing power. If the good is a significant part of a consumer's income or budget, then a change in price will be greatly felt. Choice D is the best answer because purchasing fruit does not make up a significant percentage of a person's income or budget as compared to buying and maintaining a boat.

127. (B) Choice B is the best answer because a school can hire teaching assistants very easily in the short run. Long-run adjustments are major and significant changes to a firm, such as plant size and investing in human capital.

128. (A) Choice A is the best answer because it describes the natural flow of business for a perfectly competitive firm. More firms entering the market, a decrease in price, and a decrease in long-run profits come after other firms start making an economic profit in a perfectly competitive market.

129. (B) Remember that calculating economic profit includes the opportunity costs of business decisions. Choice B is the best choice because it accounts for the opportunity cost lost in starting up a business. $70,000 – $60,000 – $3,000 = $7,000. The $3,000 is considered because that is money Danielle lost in interest from her savings account.

130. (C) If marginal revenue (MR), the same as price, is equal to average variable costs (AVC), then firms could shut down and pay only their total fixed costs (TFC). If firms shut down in the short run, then AVC does not need to be paid, only TFC.

131. (C) Since a monopoly is the sole producer of a product, the firm will charge an increased price as compared to a perfect competition, where price is established through supply and demand. Remember, in a monopoly, there is no competition, so firms will always charge a higher price.

132. (A) Choice A is the best answer because as firms grow, the tendencies are to experience an increase in costs with an increase in production. This tendency is known as diseconomies of scale.

133. (A) There are many different types of smartphones on the market produced by many different firms. Although they are similar in many ways (i.e., you can make a phone call, send a text, surf the Internet), product differentiation offers variety. Remember, if you see product differentiation, then a monopolistic competition is being discussed.

134. (B) In a perfect competition, the price of a good is established at the equilibrium point between supply and demand.

135. (C) Choice C is the best answer because tobacco is a cost of production for cigarettes. If the price increases for a cost of production, then firms must increase their price to keep making a profit on producing the good.

136. (A) Choice A is the best answer because a consumer surplus is the difference between what a consumer is willing and able to pay and the actual market price. If the consumer paid more for the product than the established market price, then there is a consumer surplus.

137. (E) Two of the major characteristics of a monopolistic competition are product differentiation and advertising. Since product differentiation exists in a monopolistic competition, firms must advertise why their product is different and better than the products of their competitors.

138. (A) Two of the major characteristics of a monopolistic competition are product differentiation and advertising. Since product differentiation exists in a monopolistic competition, firms must advertise why their product is different and better than the products of their competitors.

139. (C) If more and more firms are exiting the market, then costs must be greater than price. Choice C is the best answer because it shows that price is less than average total cost (ATC) in a perfectly competitive market structure.

140. (A) Remember that a monopolist is the only producer of a good or service and has no competition. Therefore, the firm may raise the price higher than marginal costs. All firms will maximize profit where marginal revenue (MR) equals marginal cost (MC), but a monopolist will support a higher price than the MC.

141. (B) An oligopoly and a monopoly have barriers to entry into the market. A perfect competition and a monopolistic competition are market structures that have ease of entry into the market.

142. (C) Choice C is the best answer because a firm is operating efficiently if price (P) equals marginal cost (MC). Choice B is incorrect because the government would not allow P to be greater than MC. Choices A and D represent inefficiency.

143. (A) Marginal utility is defined as the additional satisfaction or utility a consumer receives from consuming one additional unit of a good. Choice B is incorrect because it refers to the marginal revenue cost. Choice C is incorrect because it refers to the marginal propensity to save. Choice D is incorrect because it describes marginal cost. Choice E is incorrect because it describes marginal benefit.

144. (B) The law of diminishing marginal utility states that as a person increases consumption of a good, satisfaction or utility decreases with each marginal consumption of the good.

145. (B) When most people say the word *profit*, they are referring to accounting profit, calculated as the difference between total revenue and total explicit cost. Economic profit, however, calculates the opportunity cost (implicit cost). Choice B is the best answer.

146. (A) When most people say the word *profit*, they are referring to accounting profit, calculated as the difference between total revenue and total explicit cost. Economic profit, however, calculates the opportunity cost (implicit cost). In this scenario, accounting profit would be $150,000 minus $50,000. Economic profit would be $150,000 minus $50,000 minus $75,000.

147. (D) Inefficiency is the hallmark of a monopoly market structure. Since prices are higher and output lower in monopolies, resources are not being allocated in the most efficient way to benefit consumers and society.

148. (B) Price discrimination refers to a systematic pricing system that charges a different price to different groups of people. However, the firm will still ensure that the maximum price that these different people are willing to pay is utilized.

149. (A) Price discrimination allows firms to receive every dollar available from their customers. If a firm can successfully identify specific groups of people and ensure that customers do not resell their product to other consumers, then price discrimination would be successful. An example would be selling movie tickets in a theater. There are different prices for shows at different times, and different prices for different types of customers: adult, child, and senior citizen.

150. (A) Since product differentiation exists in a monopolistic competition, firms must advertise why their product is different and better than the products of their competitors. It makes more economic sense to Deirdre to buy the cheaper toy, but the power of advertising ensures that the more expensive product attracts her daughter.

151. (C) You should be aware of the graphical representation of profit for all market structures. This graph represents the profit of a monopolistic competitive firm. The shaded area represents profit because the price level is more than the average total cost (ATC). Since the ATC represents the total cost divided by the output, if the price is higher than this number, then the firm is making a profit.

152. (C) Choice C is the best answer because a monopolistic competitive market has an ease of entry into the market. If producing a product is profitable, more and more firms will enter the market, and profits will decrease and firms will break even.

153. (D) Game theory examines the relationships between participants in a specific model structure and attempts to predict their actions. This is useful for studying oligopolies because they are very large firms made up of interdependent companies, producing either a standardized or differentiated product with barriers to entry.

154. (E) Choice E is the best answer because establishing a price ceiling will not influence the price of the quantity demanded or supplied. It only ensures that producers will not exceed a specific price for their product, thus protecting consumers.

155. (D) Remember that for all market structures, the profit-maximizing point is where MR = MC. Choice D is the best answer because it reflects this relationship. In a perfectly competitive market, price will equal marginal revenue. Marginal revenue is the amount a perfectly competitive firm will receive from selling one additional unit of output. Since supply and demand set prices in a perfect competition, price will equal marginal revenue.

156. (E) Remember that for all market structures, the profit-maximizing point is where MR = MC.

157. (B) Item I is not a part of a market system, because it describes the operations of a traditional economy. Item III is not part of a market system, because it describes a command economy. Choice B is correct because Item II describes the interactions between consumers and producers.

158. (D) Price leadership refers to a firm that is a leader among its competitors and sets the market price, and others will follow along because they wish to hold on to their market share. Choice D is the best answer because an oligopoly fits this description.

159. (B) Choice B is the best answer because total variable costs are the costs that vary, or change, as the level of output changes. Choice A is incorrect because it describes fixed costs. Choice C is incorrect because it describes average fixed costs. Choice D is incorrect because it describes average variable costs.

160. (C) Choice C is the best answer because if something is implicit, then it is not blatantly seen outright. An opportunity cost is an excellent example of an implicit cost. Choice A is incorrect because it describes explicit costs. Choice B is incorrect because is describes total variable costs. Choice D is incorrect because it describes average variable costs.

161. (D) Choice D is the best answer because the complement effect refers to an increase or decrease in demand for a product that works with another product. For example, if the demand for tennis rackets increases, so will the demand for tennis balls. This reflects a direct relationship, whereas all the other choices reflect an inverse relationship.

162. (D) An increase in technology is a major change in the factors of production. If technology increases, then production output will increase as well. This will result in greater profits. However, since this is a perfectly competitive market, price will remain the same.

163. (A) Choice A is the best answer because an increase in technology is a major change in the factors of production. If technology increases, then production output will increase as well. This will result in greater profits. However, as a monopoly the firm can still increase prices because monopolies are price setters.

164. (A) Choice A is the best answer because if a firm is utilizing its resources efficiently, then price (P) will equal marginal cost (MC). Keep in mind the opposite notion: since monopolies are notoriously inefficient, they operate where P is greater than MC.

165. (C) Remember, in a perfectly competitive market as more and more firms enter the market due to no barriers to entry, prices will decrease to the point where economic profit will equal zero. This is a natural occurrence. Profit in the long run for all perfectly competitive firms will always equal zero.

166. (B) A cartel, which is a form of an oligopoly, is a market structure where there are a small number of interdependent firms, producing either a standardized or differentiated product with barriers to entry. Since these firms work together to establish prices and control supply and demand, there is always the incentive to cheat to earn a greater profit than its competitors.

167. (A) Dead weight loss refers to the lost net benefit to society caused by a movement from competitive market equilibrium. In other words, the people who would purchase the good who have more marginal benefit than marginal price are not purchasing the product. For a monopoly, this occurs when price is greater than marginal cost.

168. (E) Choice E is the best answer because $P = MR = MC = ATC$ represents a perfectly competitive firm.

169. (A) Price taking refers to firms that establish their price through the market forces of supply and demand. Since oligopolies are very large firms and work together to control supply and demand, they are price setters.

170. (A) The reason a monopoly can charge a higher price is because there are no competitors in the market. If a firm is the sole producer of a product, it will charge a higher price. Choices B and D are incorrect because they describe characteristics of a monopolistic competition.

171. (C) Price elasticity of demand is extremely useful because it helps firms and economists predict consumer behavior if there is a change in price. Choice C is the best answer.

172. (B) Remember, a price ceiling will always be demarcated below the market equilibrium price on a supply-and-demand chart.

173. (A) Calculating the cross-elasticity refers to the measurement taken of how sensitive the consumption of one good is to the change in price of another good. Choice A is the best answer.

174. (A) A normal profit is described as another way of saying a firm is earning an economic profit of zero. This is so because normal profit and economic profit calculate opportunity costs.

175. (C) Choice C is the best answer because if producing a product is profitable, more and more firms will enter the market due to the ease of entry. Remember, in the long run, the economic profits of a perfectly competitive firm will be zero.

176. (E) Choice E is the best answer because $MR = MC$ represents the profit-maximizing point for all market structures. If a firm is operating at this point, then all resources are being utilized efficiently.

177. (E) Choice E is the best answer because it describes price leadership, where one firm is a leader among its competitors and sets the market price, and others will follow along because they wish to hold on to their market share. This is very true for oligopolies.

178. (A) Remember, the profit-maximizing point will always be MR = MC for any market structure, even a cartel.

179. (A) Choices B and E are incorrect because the opposite is true due to barriers to entry. Choice C is incorrect because price discrimination is unrelated. Choice D is incorrect because it is unrelated. Choice A is the best answer because a restriction to how many firms enter the market would allow a greater opportunity for profit.

180. (B) Choice A is incorrect because it describes the substitution effect. Choice C is incorrect because it describes marginal utility. Choices D and E are incorrect because they are not related to the income effect. The correct choice is A because the income effect describes the relationship between income and demand: as a person's income increases or decreases, it will increase or decrease demand for a product.

181. (B) Remember that a perfectly competitive firm in the long run will have economic profits of zero. Normal profit will equal economic profit.

182. (B) The total revenue curve illustrates the relationship between the total revenue a firm receives for selling its product and the quantity of the product sold. The marginal revenue curve is taken directly from the total revenue curve.

183. (A) If economies of scale exist, then a monopoly could develop a cost advantage over other competitors attempting to enter the market. They might use this advantage to manipulate the price of the product. For example, a monopoly might decrease prices in order to incur losses to a competitor's firm.

184. (A) Dead weight loss refers to the lost net benefit to society caused by a movement from competitive market equilibrium. In other words, the people who would purchase the good who have more marginal benefit than marginal price are not purchasing the product.

185. (A) Average total cost (ATC) is the total cost divided by the output. If the ATC equals price (P), then firms will make an economic profit of zero.

Chapter 3: Factor Markets

186. (A) Derived demand refers to the demand for resources that come from the demand for the goods produced by the resources. Choice A is the best answer because the demand for workers comes from the demand for automobiles for consumers to drive.

187. (B) The marginal revenue product of labor (MRP) refers to the change in a firm's total revenue from hiring one additional unit of labor. The best way to calculate the MRP is to multiply the marginal product (producing one more unit of output) by the product price.

188. (D) Choice D is the best answer because the revenue product of labor (MRP) refers to the change in a firm's total revenue from hiring one additional unit of labor. All firms should hire to the point where MRP = W.

189. (C) Wages are a major cost to firms. If wages increase, then the cost of production will increase, which would shift the labor supply curve to the left.

190. (C) Remember the determinants of supply. If there is a new development in technology, it would potentially decrease the cost of production and shift the curve to the right.

191. (A) Human capital refers to the skills a worker applies on the job. Acquiring human capital increases a worker's value in the marketplace. Human capital is a major factor of production, and any increase in human capital through educational training would increase the productivity of labor.

192. (A) Remember the formula for MRP (MRP = the marginal product multiplied by the product price). To answer this question just plug in the numbers: MRP/P = MP or 40/5 = 8 hours. All other choices are miscalculations.

193. (A) Choices C, D, and E are incorrect because they would all result in an increase in demand. Choice A is the best choice because the marginal revenue product (MRP) refers to the change in a firm's total revenue from hiring one additional unit of labor. As you know, the demand curve slopes downward because of the law of demand, and the MRP curve slopes downward because as marginal product falls, so does the marginal revenue product.

194. (C) Choice C is the best answer because they all represent the determinants of labor demand. The key to answering this question is product demand: if the price of a product changes, so too will the demand. Therefore, this will influence the marginal revenue product.

195. (E) Choice E is the best answer because the question reflects some of the reasons the labor supply curve might shift. A change in taste may shift the labor supply curve. For example, a changing mentality in society for appropriate jobs for different people may change and thus change the labor supply. Immigration will affect a labor supply curve because if it decreases, it will shift that country's labor supply curve to the left.

196. (B) Choice B is the best answer because a monopsony in a factor market is where a sole firm has total market power.

197. (C) Choice C is the best answer because wheat is a factor of production for producing bagels. If the price of a factor of production decreases, Seth can increase production and his demand for labor will increase.

198. (B) Choice B is the correct answer because derived demand refers to the demand for resources that come from the demand for the goods produced by the resources. Choice A is incorrect because it refers to the demand for labor. Choice C is incorrect because it illustrates the least-cost rule. Choice D is incorrect because that is the profit-maximizing point for resource employment. Choice E is incorrect because it refers to a monopsony.

199. (A) Derived demand refers to the demand for resources that come from the demand for the goods produced by the resource. People have a demand not for the worker but for the product the worker produces. Choice A is the best answer because the demand for tractors and workers is derived from people's demand for food.

200. (C) Choice C is the best answer because many people go to the doctor when they catch a cold. If a cure is found for the common cold, people will have less doctor visits and would decrease the demand for doctors in the long run. Every other choice would increase the demand for doctors.

201. (A) The output effect states that there will be a rise in output if the price of a resource used in the production of a product decreases, and firms will increase production and the demand for labor will increase.

202. (B) Remember that the MRP curve and the demand curve are similar in that they are both downward sloping. If a firm's MRP increases, so will demand.

203. (B) Choice A is incorrect because it refers to the marginal revenue cost. Choice C is incorrect because it refers to the least-cost rule. Choice D is incorrect because it refers to profit maximizing. Choice E is incorrect because it refers to a monopsony. The marginal revenue product of labor (MRP) refers to the change in a firm's total revenue from hiring one additional unit of labor.

204. (D) If wages exceed the marginal revenue product (MRP) of labor, then firms need to lay off workers until wages and MRP are equal.

205. (A) Choice A is the best answer because the price of machinery is a factor of production. If the machinery used in the production of a product decreases in price, then firms may purchase more at lower prices, which would increase the need for labor.

206. (A) If the price of a resource used in the production of a product decreases, then a major factor of production has decreased. This would result in an increase in production and an increase in the demand for labor.

207. (C) Immigration will affect a labor supply curve because if it decreases, it will shift that country's labor supply curve to the left. The labor supply curve will shift to the right for the country the labor supply enters.

208. (C) If the factors of production increase for a firm, then prices will increase and workers need to be laid off to the point where MRP = W so the firm may still make a profit.

209. (A) Remember that complements are products that are used with another product. For example, you cannot play tennis without a racket and tennis balls. If the price of a good increases, so will the price of its complements. This will result in a decrease in labor because firms will lay off workers until MRP = W.

210. (C) Choice A is incorrect because it refers to a monopsony and the answer does not fully answer the question. Choice B is incorrect because it refers to profit maximizing. Choice D is incorrect because it refers to marginal revenue cost. Choice E is incorrect because it refers to the marginal revenue product. Choice C is the best answer because the least-cost rule seeks to find the best combination between resources and capital that would be the cheapest for the firm.

211. (A) Like any profit-maximizing firm, the equilibrium point to determine the number of workers to hire is where MRP = W.

212. (A) Choice A is the best answer because consumers do not demand the workers themselves; rather, they demand the products the workers produce. Therefore, labor is a derived demand.

213. (D) Like any profit-maximizing firm, the equilibrium point to determine the number of workers to hire is where MRP = W.

214. (B) Wages are a major cost to firms. If the price of labor increases, then firms will lay off workers to the point where MRP = W.

Chapter 4: Market Failure and the Role of Government

215. (B) Choice B is the best answer because marginal social cost (MSC) refers to the total cost to society producing one more unit in an economy. The total cost does not just reflect the cost to the producer but to the external environment.

216. (A) If a positive externality is produced, a person who does not consume or work on the product benefits from it nonetheless. This is known as a marginal external benefit (MEB). The demand curve would not reflect MEB, unless the government intervened and internalized it.

217. (A) The graph represents a shift of the demand curve to the right. Eliminate any answer that would lessen or weaken consumers' purchasing power. Choice A is the best choice because a government subsidy decreases the impact on people's wallets. This would shift the demand curve to the right.

218. (D) If a positive externality is produced, a person who does not consume or work on the product benefits from it nonetheless. This is known as a marginal external benefit (MEB). The demand curve would not reflect MEB, unless the government intervened and internalized it.

219. (A) Through regulation, the government may impose restrictions on producers, such as a tax. The graph illustrates a leftward shift of the supply curve. Therefore, eliminate any answer that incorporates a rightward shift of the supply curve. Choice A is the best answer.

220. (B) Choice B is correct because since the government intervened and shifted the supply curve to the left, production will decrease and the negative externality of overproduction will be corrected.

221. (D) A free rider is a person who benefits from goods and services without incurring any of the costs. The goal of a private firm is to earn a profit, and if free riders are enjoying the benefits of a good or service, then firms do not produce.

222. (D) An ability to pay tax is also known as a progressive tax: tax rates should vary according to one's ability to pay them. If a person or company earns a higher income, then that person or company should pay more taxes than those who make less.

223. (A) A tax is regressive if the proportion of income paid in taxes decreases as income increases. A sales tax is an example of this because people with low incomes pay a higher portion of their money on sales tax compared to people with high incomes.

224. (A) Compensating differential refers to the measurement between the unpleasantness of a job and wage. For example, a firefighter is doing a more dangerous job than a telemarketer. It does not place the value of one job over the other; it only says that these jobs are different. Although college professors may be more esteemed in the workforce due to their level of education, many plumbers earn more money. The key difference is the nonmonetary differences of a job.

225. (B) Compensating differential refers to the measurement between the unpleasantness of a job and wage. Choice B is the best answer because it refers to the characteristics of the worker, not the characteristics of the job.

226. (D) Choice D is the best answer because a person does not have to incur the costs of a radio station to enjoy the benefits of it; he or she just has to turn on the radio. Choices A, B, C, and E must be purchased by a consumer if he or she wishes to enjoy the benefits of the good or service.

227. (C) A proportional tax is a tax that is paid from someone's income regardless of income level and is also known as a "flat tax."

228. (D) Since a negative externality in the form of pollution emerged, a government intervention would focus on the producers of the pollution. Any choice that refers to a government intervention on the part of consumers may be eliminated. Choice C is incorrect because it would decrease costs for producers and may lead to an increase in production. Choice D is the best answer because a tax on producers would increase costs and result in a decrease in production and hopefully pollution.

229. (C) A proportional tax is a tax where the same proportion of income is paid in taxes regardless of income level. Anna received a raise in salary, but she still paid 20% of her income in taxes.

230. (D) A public good is a good that is nonexcludable. Choice D is the best choice because firefighters must respond to help, regardless if the person paid his or her taxes.

231. (A) A Gini ratio is a measure of income inequality. If the Gini ratio is closer to zero, income distribution is more equal. If the Gini ratio is closer to 1, income distribution is more unequal. Choice A is the best answer because this illustrates the definition of a Gini ratio.

232. (E) The diagram is called a Lorenz curve: a graph that illustrates how a nation's income is distributed throughout a nation's households.

233. (A) Refer to question 231. Choice A is the best answer because a Gini ratio of 0.9 is very close to 1; therefore, it shows a highly unequal distribution of income.

234. (E) Choice E is the best answer because this scenario represents a regressive tax. A regressive tax is a tax where the proportion of income paid in taxes decreases as income rises. There is a big difference in salaries between Anna and Sarah, yet Sarah pays only $2,000 more in taxes than Anna.

235. (A) Choice A is the best answer because a free market system, without any aid in government intervention, often results in unequal distribution of wealth.

236. (A) A regressive tax is a tax where the proportion of income paid in taxes decreases as income rises. Choice B is incorrect because a proportional tax is a tax that is paid from someone's income regardless of income level. Choice C is incorrect because a flat tax is the same as a proportional tax. Choice D is incorrect because a progressive tax is a tax where the proportion of income paid in taxes increases as income increases. Choice E is incorrect because a tax bracket is based on a person's income level: as your income increases, then you might fall into a tax bracket that pays higher taxes.

237. (A) A progressive tax is a tax where the proportion of income paid in taxes increases as income increases. See question 236.

238. (B) A private good is a good that can rival other goods and is excludable to other consumers. If a person does not have the money to pay for a taxicab ride, then he or she is forced to find another mode of transportation.

239. (D) Since the world benefited from this satellite transmission, the satellite is a public good. A public good is a good that is nonexcludable.

240. (C) Choice C is the best answer because taxes like a progressive tax help with the redistribution of wealth. Choice D is incorrect because it does not differentiate income levels on the percentage of tax paid. Choice A is incorrect because other economic systems help in the redistribution of wealth, such as a mixed economic system.

241. (C) Choice C is the best answer because the spillover effect refers to additional benefits to society from the production of a good. Chris's neighbors all benefit from Chris's work without incurring any of the costs.

242. (E) If a good is produced that not all people enjoy the benefit of, it is known as a private good. A private good is a good that can rival other goods and is excludable to other consumers. For example, if a person does not have the money to pay for a taxicab ride, then he or she is forced to find another mode of transportation.

243. (A) A public good is a good that is nonexcludable. For example, firefighters must respond to help, regardless if the person paid his or her taxes.

244. (C) Taxes such as a progressive tax help with the redistribution of wealth.

245. (B) A negative externality refers to costs in the production of goods and services that are put upon a third party. For example, pollution is an example of a negative externality. Therefore, any answer that describes a benefit to society should be eliminated. Choice B is the best answer. Choice A is incorrect because it describes egalitarianism.

246. (C) A free rider is a person who benefits from goods and services without incurring any of the costs. The goal of a private firm is to earn a profit, and if free riders are enjoying the benefits of a good or service, then firms do not produce.

247. (C) A positive externality refers to the benefits experienced by a third party outside the production of a good or service. Therefore, any choice that describes a cost to society should be eliminated. Choice A is incorrect because it describes egalitarianism.

248. (A) If a negative externality exists, then production costs are being placed on a third party outside of production. If a firm overallocates its resources, then they are not being utilized efficiently and may result in negative externality. Choice B is incorrect because there would be no benefit in the form of a positive externality from overallocating resources. Choice C is incorrect because the government would not subsidize spillover costs for a firm. Choice D is incorrect because we have no way of knowing what the shutdown point is without more information.

249. (B) Items III and IV are private goods in that they are rival and excludable. If someone purchases a bean burrito, the only person who benefits is the person who eats it and the company that sold it to him. Firefighters and traffic lights are public goods and services because all benefit regardless of payment of taxes.

250. (A) Some of the powers of the government to help the economy grow and be competitive are regulation and antitrust laws. In a completely free market, there is a risk of firms creating monopolies on the market. The government ensures competition (which ensures reasonable prices for goods and services) through regulation and antitrust laws.

Macroeconomics

CHAPTER 5

Basic Economic Concepts

1. The study of macroeconomics refers to

    (A) the part of economics that deals with large-scale economic concepts, like interest rates and gross national product

    (B) the part of economics that deals with how individuals and business firms allocate scarce resources

    (C) economic theory that stresses costs of production and small-business scale decisions

    (D) the difference between normative and positive economics

    (E) all of the above

Refer to the following graph to answer question 2.

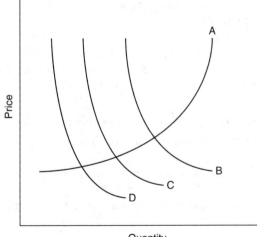

2. According to the preceding diagram, the relationship between price and quantity is illustrated by line
   (A) A
   (B) B
   (C) C
   (D) D
   (E) A and B

3. Ronald wants to buy an Xbox. According to the laws of economics, Ronald will buy the Xbox if
   (A) the opportunity cost is less than the purchase costs
   (B) the marginal benefit is greater than the marginal cost
   (C) the marginal cost is greater than the marginal benefit
   (D) the marginal benefit is equal to the marginal cost
   (E) none of the above

4. A country is said to have a comparative advantage over another country when
   (A) it can produce a good at a lower opportunity cost than another country
   (B) it can produce a good utilizing fewer resources per unit of output than another country
   (C) there is a higher degree of specialization and division of labor compared to another country
   (D) when comparing each country's production possibilities frontiers, one country is operating at maximum efficiency and output
   (E) one country's production possibilities frontier is shifted farther to the right compared to another country's production possibilities frontier

5. Which of the following statements applies only to macroeconomics?
   (A) Minimum wage should be increased to give more people disposable income.
   (B) New technology will cause a shift in the demand curve.
   (C) The demand for cell phones is elastic.
   (D) Foreign imports and increasing wage demands are contributing to price inflation.
   (E) The demand for gasoline is inelastic.

6. It is beneficial for two countries to trade only when there is/are
    (A) a mutually beneficial trade agreement
    (B) increasing returns to scale
    (C) decreasing returns to scale
    (D) an absolute advantage in production between the two countries
    (E) a comparative advantage in production between the two countries

7. Any point along the production possibilities curve is
    (A) attainable and efficient
    (B) attainable yet inefficient
    (C) unattainable and inefficient
    (D) showing that resources are not being utilized to their full potential
    (E) none of the above

8. Economic growth refers to
    (A) a rightward shift of the production possibilities curve
    (B) movement along the demand curve
    (C) movement along the supply curve
    (D) the point where the supply and demand curves intersect
    (E) the allocation of private property into public sectors

9. The production possibilities curve is concave because
    (A) as production of goods and services increases, the opportunity costs decrease
    (B) taxes increase as the production of a good increases
    (C) as production of goods and services increases, the opportunity costs increase
    (D) both B and C
    (E) both A and C

10. Tommy has two free hours to do whatever he would like. He thinks of the many activities he might engage in and settles on a choice between tutoring his younger brother in AP Economics or sitting and watching television. His parents pay him $10 per hour when he helps his brother study. He chooses to sit and watch television for two hours. The opportunity cost of this decision is
    (A) $20, because opportunity cost is the next best alternative given up when a decision is made
    (B) $0, because the marginal benefit is greater than the marginal cost of watching television
    (C) $10, because the marginal benefit is greater than the marginal cost of watching television
    (D) $0, because the opportunity cost is the next best alternative given up when a decision is made
    (E) none of the above

11. Your school decides to build a new performing arts center. What is the opportunity cost of constructing the new performing arts center?
    (A) The money used for the construction of the performing arts center
    (B) The cost of building the performing arts center now, rather than waiting until next year
    (C) Any other good or service that now cannot be provided due to the resources used for the new performing arts center
    (D) Without the knowledge of the next best option for using the resources that went to the performing arts center, the answer cannot be known
    (E) None of the above

12. Both of the economies of the fictional nations Reilly and Tanen have the same production possibilities curve. They both are operating at the same point on the curve. If Tanen discovers a new resource for production, the most likely result of the production possibilities curves would be
    (A) Tanen's curve would shift to the right, whereas Reilly's would stay the same
    (B) both Tanen's and Reilly's curve would shift to the right
    (C) Tanen's curve would shift to the right, whereas Reilly's would shift to the left
    (D) Tanen's curve would stay the same, whereas Reilly's would shift to the left
    (E) none of the above

13. If a society *overallocates* its resources, then
    (A) consumer spending would increase due to an increase in demand
    (B) marginal benefit would be greater than marginal cost
    (C) the opportunity cost of producing one more unit would increase exponentially
    (D) marginal benefit would be less than marginal cost
    (E) marginal benefit would equal marginal cost

14. All of the following are examples of a market economy EXCEPT
    (A) competition among sellers of products
    (B) government ownership of the factors of production
    (C) freedom of sellers to enter and exit the market
    (D) unrestricted consumer choice
    (E) the existence of markets

15. The boundary between attainable and unattainable outputs is represented by
    (A) the Laffer curve
    (B) the Phillips curve
    (C) the equilibrium point between supply and demand
    (D) the point of diminishing returns
    (E) the production possibilities curve

16. "Scarcity" is best defined as
    (A) material resources that are limited
    (B) an idea used by industrializing nations to satisfy unlimited wants and desires with limited natural resources
    (C) limited vital material resources compared with limited wants and needs
    (D) all points lying outside the production possibilities curve
    (E) the idea that a society's wants and needs are unlimited, and material resources are limited

17. Both Luca and Sarah can weed the garden and walk their dog on Sunday morning. For every half hour of walking the dog, Luca can weed twice the amount of garden Sarah can. According to this information,

    (A) Sarah walks the dog because she has absolute advantage in weeding the garden
    (B) Luca walks the dog because he has comparative advantage in weeding the garden
    (C) Luca weeds the garden because he has comparative advantage in weeding the garden
    (D) Sarah weeds the garden because she has comparative advantage in weeding the garden
    (E) Sarah walks the dog because she has comparative advantage in walking the dog

18. Joe is in training, hoping he will make the varsity football team next season. He will usually train for five hours a day, four days a week. On the last day of training before tryouts, Joe decides to train one extra hour. Joe's decision is worth it if which of the following is TRUE?

    (A) Joe should continue training for an extra hour if he thinks the extra practice will help him get on the team.
    (B) Joe should continue training an extra hour if the marginal cost is greater than the marginal benefit.
    (C) Joe should continue training an extra hour if the marginal benefit is greater than the marginal cost.
    (D) Joe should not continue training an extra hour, because the opportunity cost is too great.
    (E) Joe should not continue training an extra hour, because the opportunity cost is equal to the decision to train.

19. The significant difference between supply and aggregate supply is

    (A) supply is the total amount of a good that is available to consumers; aggregate supply is the total supply of goods in an economy
    (B) supply is the total supply of goods available in an economy; aggregate supply is the total amount of a good available to consumers
    (C) supply is the total amount of a good that is available to consumers; aggregate supply is the total amount of goods demanded and supplied in an economy
    (D) supply is the total amount of a good demanded by consumers; aggregate supply is the total amount of goods demanded and supplied by producers
    (E) none of the above

20. Mineral deposits, human capital, entrepreneurship, use of technology, and machinery are all examples of

(A) factors of production
(B) superior and inferior goods
(C) elements sometimes needed to move an existing company overseas
(D) public goods
(E) material wants and needs

21. Which of the following will cause an outward shift of the production possibilities curve?

(A) Cuts in funding in educational training for employees
(B) A decrease in a nation's birthrate, thus decreasing the labor force
(C) A natural disaster creating extreme limitations of a vital natural resource
(D) An increase in skilled workers
(E) None of the above

22. The term *ceteris paribus* means

(A) if event A precedes event B, A caused B
(B) economics deals with facts, not values
(C) other things equal
(D) prosperity inevitably follows recession
(E) out of many one

23. How is it possible for a country to obtain more than its production possibilities curve dictates?

(A) Not possible without greater quantities of the factors of production already obtained
(B) Specialization and trade
(C) Increase in education and job training
(D) Obtainment of a greater quantity of affordable substitutes
(E) Increase in the division of labor

24. The production possibilities curve will show a straight line if which of the following is TRUE?

(A) The opportunity cost is constant.
(B) Vital resources for the good are limitless.
(C) The economy is operating below maximum efficiency and output.
(D) The law of decreasing marginal utility does not apply.
(E) Marginal benefit is less than marginal cost.

25. According to the law of demand,
    (A) as the price of a good or service increases, the demand will shift to the right
    (B) as the price of a good or service increases, the demand will shift to the left
    (C) there is an inverse relationship between quantity demanded of a good or service and the price of that good or service
    (D) as prices for a good or service increase, consumers will begin to use complementary goods
    (E) as the price of a good or service increases, the quantity demanded will increase

26. Within the market system, prices are determined by
    (A) supply and demand
    (B) a central planning committee
    (C) opportunity cost
    (D) aggregate demand
    (E) the Federal Reserve

27. Suppose a very dry and hot season contributes to a poor yield of tobacco for the year. As a result, the low supply of tobacco increases the price of cigarettes. What could be said regarding the price elasticity of cigarettes?
    (A) Cigarettes are price inelastic, and demand will remain the same.
    (B) Cigarettes are price inelastic, and demand will decrease.
    (C) Cigarettes are price elastic, as there are other alternatives to smoking.
    (D) Cigarettes are price elastic, and the demand will decrease.
    (E) None of the above

28. If the demand for bowling balls increases, what could be said regarding bowling shoes?
    (A) The demand for bowling shoes will decrease.
    (B) The demand for bowling shoes will increase.
    (C) The price of bowling shoes will decrease.
    (D) The quantity supplied will decrease.
    (E) None of the above

29. Without government regulations, the equilibrium price is established

 (A) at the next price above where the demand and supply curves intersect
 (B) when the quantity supplied equals the quantity demanded
 (C) at the next price below where the demand and supply curves intersect
 (D) when you take the difference between the two lowest points plotted on the demand and supply curves
 (E) at the price where either the demand or supply curve becomes horizontal

30. All of the following are examples of macroeconomic variables EXCEPT

 (A) the price of skateboards sold in the United States between 1995 and 2005
 (B) the percentage change in income levels in Kenya between 1980 and 2000
 (C) the gross exports of goods out of the United Kingdom in 2010
 (D) the average price level of goods in the United States in 2011
 (E) the unemployment rate in Germany after World War I

CHAPTER 6

Measurement of Economic Systems

31. The circular flow model illustrates

(A) that workers, entrepreneurs, and owners of land and capital offer their services through product markets

(B) the structures of both command and capitalist economic systems

(C) that workers, entrepreneurs, and owners of land and capital offer their services through national agencies

(D) how the Federal Reserve buys and sells bonds to stimulate the economy

(E) that workers, entrepreneurs, and owners of land and capital offer their services through a resource market

32. In the simple circular flow model

(A) individuals and householders are sellers of resources and demanders of products

(B) householders are sellers of products and demanders of resources

(C) the GDP is represented by the number of households and businesses in the economy

(D) businesses are sellers of resources and demanders of products

(E) businesses are sellers of products and sellers of resources

33. If you wanted to understand the relationship between households, businesses, and resources, you would study

(A) the circular flow model

(B) the equilibrium point of supply and demand

(C) nonmarket transactions

(D) aggregate supply

(E) aggregate demand

34. When economists refers to the gross domestic product (GDP), they mean
    (A) all final goods and services produced in an economy in a year
    (B) all intermediate and final goods and services produced in an economy in a year
    (C) all final goods and services produced in an economy in a five-year time period
    (D) all final goods and services produced in an economy in a year, including overseas branches and divisions
    (E) the total expenditure of consumer and government spending in an economy in a given year

35. The most significant difference between gross domestic product and gross national product would be
    (A) government spending
    (B) consumer income
    (C) net income from foreign investments
    (D) consumer spending minus government investments
    (E) A and C

36. The amounts businesses are willing and able to invest at each possible level of GDP is known as the
    (A) investment schedule
    (B) aggregate supply schedule
    (C) aggregate demand schedule
    (D) nominal rate of interest
    (E) marginal propensity to consume

37. Which of the following are considered leakages from the circular flow model?
    (A) Taxes and savings
    (B) Taxes and the price of capital goods
    (C) Savings and the price of natural resources
    (D) Taxes and interest rates
    (E) Interest rates and automatic stabilizers

38. An example of a final good calculated into the GDP for the year would be
    (A) a computer chip bought by IBM to be used in a computer
    (B) a used car sold to a consumer
    (C) a new car sold to a consumer
    (D) the lumber used to construct a new house
    (E) all of the above

39. Housing, education, and health insurance are goods and services that have what in common?

(A) They are all provided in part by consumers and producers.

(B) They are provided only by producers.

(C) They are provided only by the government.

(D) They are provided solely by the private sector.

(E) They are provided solely by the public sector.

40. An example of an intermediate good would be

(A) a new car sold to a consumer

(B) a car engine

(C) a new laptop

(D) a new textbook to use for a college class

(E) all of the above

41. All of the following would be included in the expenditure approach to calculate GDP EXCEPT

(A) consumer spending

(B) government investments

(C) private investments

(D) consumer spending and savings

(E) net exports

42. The fact that the government is included in the circular flow model shows that the government

(A) provides goods and services to businesses and households

(B) maintains a strong control on economic resources and sells a portion of them on the open market

(C) obtains revenues in the open market

(D) does not provide goods and services to businesses and households

(E) A, B, and C only

43. The formula for calculating gross domestic product is

(A) $C - I + G + (X - M)$

(B) $C + I + G - (X + M)$

(C) $C + G + (X - M)$

(D) $(C + G)(I + ((X - M))$

(E) $C + I + G + (X - M)$

44. Jason and Mary purchased a new house in 2012 for $300,000. This purchase would be included in the GDP as
    (A) consumer savings
    (B) government investment
    (C) investment
    (D) consumption of private fixed capital
    (E) consumer spending

45. In 2011, the U.S. economy saw the value of investments rise from $150 billion to $250 billion. In calculating total investment for GDP for that year, national income accountants would
    (A) decrease GDP by $100 billion
    (B) increase GDP by $100 billion
    (C) decrease GDP by $250 billion
    (D) increase GDP by $50 billion
    (E) there would be no change in GDP for that year

Use the following data to answer question 46. The information is in billions of dollars.

Personal consumption	$1,000
Personal taxes	$10
U.S. exports	$150
U.S. imports	$175
Contributions to Social Security	$200
Private domestic investments	$350
Government investments	$600
Corporate income tax	$35

46. Based on the information in the preceding chart, the GDP would be calculated as
    (A) $1,975 billion
    (B) $2,150 billion
    (C) $2,500 billion
    (D) $1,675 billion
    (E) $1,950 billion

47. The most significant difference between nominal GDP and real GDP would be

    (A) the value of current production at the current prices
    (B) expressing the changing value of prices over time
    (C) using prices from a fixed point in time
    (D) utilizing the consumer price index
    (E) calculating fluctuations in stock market prices

48. If the nominal GDP for 2011 was $200 billion and the price index was 90, real GDP would be calculated as

    (A) $290 billion
    (B) $210 billion
    (C) $245 billion
    (D) $222 billion
    (E) $240 billion

49. Joe recently graduated from college with a degree in history. He is discouraged that he will not find a job due to tough economic times. He decides not to actively pursue a job but to wait for the economy to turn for the better. Joe is considered

    (A) structurally unemployed
    (B) frictionally unemployed
    (C) cyclically unemployed
    (D) seasonally unemployed
    (E) not part of the labor force

50. The labor force is defined as

    (A) individuals who are working or looking for a job
    (B) the percentage of people who are not working
    (C) individuals who are working, looking for a job, or not working and not looking for a job
    (D) all individuals who are working or looking for work divided by the number of people cyclically unemployed
    (E) individuals who work at least 15 hours per week

51. Elaine quit her job as a teaching assistant and went back to school to be a guidance counselor. Last year she received her master's degree and is currently looking for a job. Elaine is considered

    (A) cyclically unemployed
    (B) frictionally unemployed
    (C) structurally unemployed
    (D) seasonally unemployed
    (E) not part of the labor force

52. Full employment occurs when
    (A) cyclical unemployment does not exist
    (B) seasonal unemployment does not exist
    (C) frictional unemployment does not exist
    (D) structural unemployment does not exist
    (E) both cyclical and frictional unemployment do not exist

53. Two good measures of inflation are the
    (A) consumer price index and the natural rate of unemployment
    (B) consumer price index and the producer price index
    (C) producer price index and the natural rate of unemployment
    (D) consumer price index and the rate of stagflation
    (E) producer price index and the rate of stagflation

54. Stagflation occurs when
    (A) real GDP increases and price levels decrease
    (B) real GDP decreases and price levels decrease
    (C) unemployment and price levels increase
    (D) nominal GDP decreases and price levels increase
    (E) GDP decreases and the price level decreases

55. If a teacher loses his or her job due to low student enrollment, he or she would be considered
    (A) cyclically unemployed
    (B) seasonally unemployed
    (C) frictionally unemployed
    (D) structurally unemployed
    (E) not part of the labor force

Refer to the following chart to answer questions 56 and 57.

Employed	8,000
Unemployed	1,000
Not in the labor force	500

56. According to the chart, what is the unemployment rate?
    (A) 1.1%
    (B) 0.01%
    (C) 11%
    (D) 1.75%
    (E) 1.5%

57. According to the chart, what is the size of the labor force?

(A) 7,500

(B) 9,000

(C) 9,500

(D) 6,500

(E) The size is unknowable because the number of cyclically unemployed workers is not given.

58. Cycling Cyclist Inc. has an inventory of 100 bicycles. Last year they sold 90 bikes for $50 per bicycle. What is the value of output that would be included in the GDP for last year?

(A) $5,000

(B) $4,000

(C) $450

(D) $50,000

(E) $4,500

59. John is a supply-side economist. If the United States is experiencing stagflation, which of the following actions would he be most willing to support?

(A) The federal government increasing investment and spending

(B) An increase to the money supply

(C) The federal government decreasing investment and spending

(D) Decreasing income tax rates for the wealthy

(E) None of the above

60. Dennis decides to loan his friend some money. He would like to see a 5% return on the loan. If the current rate of inflation is 15%, what should he charge as an interest rate?

(A) 10%

(B) 20%

(C) 25%

(D) 3%

(E) 12%

61. McDonald's fast-food restaurant is an American-based industry but has franchises all over the world. The value of the output produced by a McDonald's restaurant in England is

    I.   not included in the GDP for the United States
   II. included in the GDP for the United States
  III. included in England's GDP
  IV. included in the GNP for the United States

   (A) I only
   (B) I and IV
   (C) II and III
   (D) II and IV
   (E) I, III, and IV

62. Jessica received her college degree in computer science and was offered a job at IBM. She decides to take a year off and travel throughout Europe. What would this decision do to the unemployment rate?

   (A) An increase in the unemployment rate
   (B) A decrease in the unemployment rate
   (C) An increase in cyclical unemployment
   (D) A decrease in structural unemployment
   (E) No change in the unemployment rate

63. A person who is neither working nor looking for work is considered to be

   (A) frictionally unemployed
   (B) unemployed
   (C) structurally unemployed
   (D) part of the labor force
   (E) outside of the labor force

64. Hyperinflation refers to

   (A) a rapid increase in prices
   (B) a gradual increase in prices
   (C) a rapid increase in prices, but money remains a good store of value
   (D) a decline in real GDP and an increase in the overall price level
   (E) a decrease in GDP for a continuous period of six months

65. Suppose the gross domestic product is $15 million, where consumer spending is $4 million, investments are $2 million, government spending is $5 million, and exports are $4 million. How much is spent on imports?

(A) $2 million
(B) $3 million
(C) $5 million
(D) $4 million
(E) $0

66. All of the following would be calculated into the GDP EXCEPT

(A) the sale of marshmallows to an ice-cream producer
(B) the sale of a new car
(C) the sale of an import within America's borders
(D) government purchasing weapons for the military
(E) a person paying rent for an apartment

67. When constructing a price index, a base year refers to

(A) the average price level of goods and services
(B) a point of reference to compare real values over time
(C) the percentage change in the price index over time
(D) the top of the business cycle signaling the end of expansion
(E) a collection of goods and services that represent what is consumed in an economy for the year

68. All of the following are examples of an underground economy EXCEPT

(A) selling illegal drugs
(B) paying cash to a babysitter
(C) bartering
(D) buying a used car from a car dealership
(E) a person taking a second job off the books

69. Nominal GDP refers to

(A) the value of current production, but using prices from a set point in time
(B) the value of current production, but using prices gathered over the past five years
(C) the value of current production at current prices
(D) prices at the peak of the business cycle
(E) the value of current production at the trough of the business cycle subtracted from that at the peak of the business cycle

CHAPTER 7

National Income and Price Determination

70. The aggregate demand curve slopes downward because

  (A) a higher price level makes production costs increase
  (B) it shows the amount of real output that will be purchased at each possible price level
  (C) the amount of expenditures to each production unit illustrates the amount of output
  (D) production costs decline as real output increases
  (E) both A and B

71. The aggregate demand curve is downward sloping because of

  (A) the real-balances effect
  (B) the interest rate effect
  (C) the substitute effect
  (D) the crowding out effect
  (E) both A and B

Use the following diagram to answer question 72.

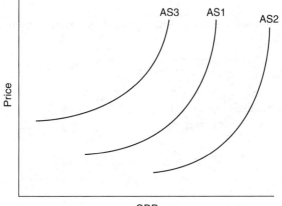

72. According to the preceding diagram, the most favorable shift of the aggregate supply curve in an economy would be
    (A) AS1 to AS2
    (B) AS1 to AS3
    (C) AS2 to AS3
    (D) AS3 to AS1
    (E) cannot be determined without knowing the aggregate demand curve

73. 0% unemployment, or when all individuals who are willing and able to work are employed, is known as
    (A) full employment
    (B) the equilibrium price at full employment
    (C) the velocity of money
    (D) the quantity theory of money
    (E) cost-push inflation

74. The gross domestic product is calculated in a way to avoid
    (A) double counting
    (B) clashes between the income and expenditure approach
    (C) discrepancies between real and nominal wages
    (D) discrepancies between real and nominal GDP
    (E) economic fluctuations

75. The multiplier effect refers to
    (A) government regulations that affect the GDP
    (B) any change in aggregate expenditures always decreases GDP
    (C) any change in aggregate expenditures creates a bigger change in GDP
    (D) the MPS will always be greater than 1
    (E) none of the above

76. All of the following will cause the aggregate demand curve to shift EXCEPT
    (A) change in consumer income
    (B) change in price level
    (C) a decrease in government spending
    (D) an increase in net exports
    (E) an increase in net imports

77. Which of the following factors will shift the aggregate supply curve to the right?
    (A) An increase in productivity
    (B) Increased wages for workers
    (C) An increase in government regulations
    (D) Consumer income increases
    (E) None of the above

78. The aggregate supply curve
    (A) is best explained by the interest rate effect
    (B) shows the amount of real output that producers are willing and able to produce at each price level
    (C) is upward sloping because of the real balances effect
    (D) reflects the amount of real output that consumers are willing and able to purchase at each price level
    (E) becomes vertical in the short run

79. Other things being equal, a shift of the aggregate supply curve to the left involves all of the following EXCEPT
    (A) an increase in government regulation
    (B) a decrease in workers' wages
    (C) a decrease in the labor force
    (D) an increase in taxes
    (E) a decrease in productivity

80. The interest rate effect suggests
    (A) a decrease in the money supply will increase interest rates
    (B) an increase in the price level will decrease the demand for money
    (C) an increase in the price level will lead consumers and businesses to borrow more money, which increases the interest rate
    (D) a decrease in the price level will lead consumers and businesses to borrow more money, which increases the interest rate
    (E) an increase in the price level will lead consumers and businesses to borrow less money, which increases the interest rate

81. The multiplier effect will be greater on aggregate demand if
    (A) there is no increase in the price level
    (B) both aggregate demand and aggregate supply increase
    (C) both aggregate demand and aggregate supply decrease
    (D) aggregate demand increases and aggregate supply decreases
    (E) cannot be determined because the up-to-date foreign exchange rate is not given

82. Imagine that investment increases by $10 billion and the MPC is 0.8. The aggregate demand curve will shift
   (A) leftward by $30 billion at each price level
   (B) rightward by $5 billion at each price level
   (C) rightward by $80 billion at each price level
   (D) leftward by $18 billion at each price level
   (E) rightward by $50 billion at each price level

83. Inflation will most likely occur when
   (A) aggregate supply and aggregate demand increase
   (B) aggregate supply and aggregate demand decrease
   (C) aggregate supply decreases and aggregate demand increases
   (D) aggregate supply increases and aggregate demand decreases
   (E) a price ceiling is placed above the equilibrium point between aggregate supply and aggregate demand

84. When aggregate demand decreases, many businesses may choose to reduce employment over reducing wages because
   (A) of restrictions over minimum wage laws
   (B) it increases the cost of production
   (C) it may create inflation
   (D) it may reduce demand for their product
   (E) competitors will lower their prices

85. Which of the following describes the aggregate supply curve in the long run?
   (A) It is horizontal.
   (B) It is always vertical.
   (C) It is upward sloping.
   (D) It is downward sloping.
   (E) It is horizontal at first, then becomes upward sloping.

86. Stagflation occurs when
   (A) aggregate demand increases and aggregate supply remains the same
   (B) aggregate demand remains the same and aggregate supply increases
   (C) there is a shock to aggregate supply
   (D) aggregate demand and aggregate supply increase
   (E) none of the above

87. Macroeconomic equilibrium occurs when
    (A) full-employment GDP exceeds equilibrium GDP
    (B) equilibrium GDP exceeds full-employment GDP
    (C) the quantity of real output demanded is equal to the quantity of real output supplied
    (D) there is a sustained falling price level
    (E) GDP falls for a consecutive six months

88. All of the following will decrease real GDP EXCEPT
    (A) an increase in government spending
    (B) an increase in the interest rate
    (C) a decrease in consumer income
    (D) a decrease in net exports
    (E) all the above choices will decrease real GDP

89. When the full-employment level exceeds the level of aggregate expenditures, which of the following most likely develops?
    (A) An inflationary gap
    (B) A recessionary gap
    (C) Hyperinflation
    (D) Stagflation
    (E) Recession

90. The biggest difference between the Phillips curve in the short run and the Phillips curve in the long run is
    (A) an indirect relationship between inflation and unemployment in the short run, and a constant relationship in the long run
    (B) a constant relationship between inflation and unemployment in the short run, and an indirect relationship in the long run
    (C) a constant relationship between inflation and unemployment both in the short run and in the long run
    (D) a direct relationship between inflation and unemployment in the short run, and a constant relationship in the long run
    (E) a constant relationship between inflation and unemployment in the long run, and a positive relationship in the short run

91. The Phillips curve examines the relationship between
    (A) aggregate demand and aggregate supply
    (B) fiscal policy and monetary policy
    (C) inflation and unemployment
    (D) inflation and cyclical unemployment
    (E) recessionary gaps and inflationary gaps

92. The full-employment equilibrium occurs at the intersection of

    (A) the aggregate demand curve and the short-run and long-run aggregate supply curves
    (B) the Phillips curve and the aggregate demand curve
    (C) the aggregate demand curve and the long-run aggregate supply curve
    (D) the aggregate demand curve and the short-run aggregate supply curve
    (E) none of the above

93. A change in spending may generate even larger or smaller changes in real GDP. This is known as the

    (A) crowding out effect
    (B) velocity of money
    (C) quantity theory of money
    (D) multiplier effect
    (E) marginal propensity to save

94. If the government increases spending by $5 billion dollars and the MPC is 0.7, what would happen to real GDP?

    (A) Increase by $15 billion
    (B) Increase by $16.5 billion
    (C) Decrease by $16.5 billion
    (D) Decrease by $15 billion
    (E) Remain the same

95. The crowding out effect refers to the relationship between

    (A) government spending/borrowing and private investment/ consumption
    (B) full-employment and inflation
    (C) unemployment and inflation
    (D) government spending/borrowing and net exports/imports
    (E) none of the above

96. Which of the following will cause the aggregate demand curve to shift to the right?

    (A) An increase in the price level
    (B) An increase in interest rates
    (C) An increase in government spending
    (D) A decrease in government spending
    (E) A decrease in personal consumption

97. Which of the following illustrates a positive supply shock?

    (A) Discovery of new supplies of a natural resource
    (B) A decrease in a natural resource
    (C) A decrease in the labor force over a three-year period
    (D) A decrease in the price of labor
    (E) All of the above

98. An increase in investment spending will

    (A) generate more of an increase in income due to the multiplier effect
    (B) generate less income due to the multiplier effect
    (C) generate less of an increase in income due to the net export effect
    (D) generate more of an increase in income due to the net export effect
    (E) generate more of an increase in income due to the interest rate effect

Refer to the following diagrams to answer question 99.

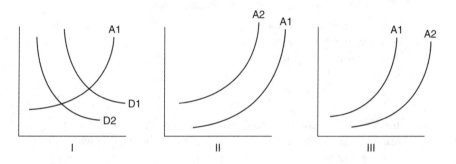

99. Which of the preceding diagrams depict(s) a negative supply shock?

    (A) Diagram I
    (B) Diagram II
    (C) Both Diagrams I and II
    (D) Both Diagrams I and III
    (E) Both Diagrams II and III

100. The best explanation why the aggregate supply curve is vertical in the long run is

    (A) enough time has passed for input prices to adjust to market forces
    (B) price level and output become equal
    (C) price level and full employment become equal
    (D) output and full employment become equal
    (E) the price of goods and services changes

101. Gross domestic product is the best indicator of

(A) national income
(B) the strength of the consumer price index
(C) the strength of the Federal Reserve Bank
(D) the strength of the producer price index
(E) all of the above

102. If the MPC is 0.6 and spending increases by $10 billion, income will

(A) increase by $60 billion
(B) decrease by $60 billion
(C) increase by $25 billion
(D) increase by $2.5 billion
(E) remain the same

103. If the President of the United States wanted to measure inflation from 2003 to 2010, he or she would most likely examine the

(A) gross national product
(B) consumer price index
(C) Federal Reserve Bank
(D) gross domestic product
(E) all of the above

104. If the United States experienced another depression on the scale of the Great Depression of the 1930s, the government should take which of the following actions?

(A) Decrease government spending
(B) Increase government spending
(C) Increase taxes and increase government spending
(D) Decrease taxes
(E) None of the above

105. If the MPC is 0.6, how much would the government need to spend if it desired a $25 billion dollar increase in national income?

(A) $2.5 billion
(B) $50 billion
(C) $15 billion
(D) $5.2 billion
(E) $10 billion

CHAPTER 8

Financial Sector

106. Jay wants to buy a new drum set for his band. He goes to two music stores over the weekend to compare prices. For Jay, money is functioning as

    (A) a unit of account
    (B) a medium of exchange
    (C) a store of value
    (D) a checkable deposit
    (E) M2 money

107. The best advantage in using money rather than a bartering system is its use as a

    (A) unit of account
    (B) medium of exchange
    (C) store of value
    (D) divisible system into M1, M2, and M3 money
    (E) method to incur and pay back loans and debt

108. Which of the following would be considered a major component of the money supply M1?

    (A) Money market accounts
    (B) Checkable deposits
    (C) Bonds
    (D) Savings deposits
    (E) All of the above

109. Anna recently celebrated her 18th birthday. In many of her birthday cards, she found slips of paper from the U.S. government promising to repay a loan at a fixed interest rate. These slips of paper are known as

    (A) stocks
    (B) bank loans
    (C) shares
    (D) bonds
    (E) collateral

Use the following information to answer questions 110 and 111:
- I. mutual funds
- II. savings deposits
- III. currency held by consumers
- IV. checkable deposits
- V. money market deposit accounts

110. According to the preceding list of items, which are considered to be part of the M1 money supply?

(A) I and II
(B) III and V
(C) I and V
(D) IV and V
(E) III and IV

111. According to the preceding list of items, which are considered to be part of the M3 money supply?

(A) I and II
(B) I, II, and III
(C) I, II, III, and IV
(D) I, II, III, IV, and V
(E) IV and V

·112. Jacob transfers $2,000 from his savings account to his checking account. What effect will this transfer have on the M1, M2, and M3 money supply?

(A) M1 will increase, M2 decrease, and M3 will have no change.
(B) M1 will increase; M2 and M3 will remain the same.
(C) M1 will increase, M2 will remain the same, and M3 will decrease.
(D) M1 will increase, M2 will increase, and M3 will increase.
(E) The answer cannot be determined, because the total checkable deposits in the economy is not given.

113. The United States backing of the money supply comes from

(A) issuing Federal Reserve notes
(B) using land and other natural resources as collateral
(C) protecting deposits at financial institutions with deposit guarantees
(D) backing by large quantities of precious metals such as gold and silver to cover the amount of paper money in circulation
(E) all of the above

114. If the consumer price index was 90 in 2011 and five years later in 2016 it was 120, the purchasing power of the U.S. dollar fell by
    (A) 25%
    (B) 75%
    (C) 100%
    (D) 50%
    (E) 125%

115. If the interest rate decreased, there would be a
    (A) increase in the amount of money held in assets
    (B) decrease in the amount of money held in assets
    (C) increase in the demand for money
    (D) decrease in the demand for money
    (E) no change in the amount of money held in assets

116. The price of bonds and interest rates are
    (A) positively related
    (B) negatively related
    (C) unrelated
    (D) directly related
    (E) cannot be determined because the CPI for the year is not given

117. The main function of the Federal Open Market Committee is
    (A) buying and selling of securities to control the money supply
    (B) monitoring the Federal Reserve banks
    (C) monitoring the checkable deposits of commercial banks
    (D) buying and selling government bonds
    (E) monitoring the fluctuations in the money supply

118. Consumers will tend to purchase more goods and services using credit if
    (A) interest rates are increased
    (B) interest rates are decreased
    (C) the marginal propensity to save (MPS) is decreased
    (D) the marginal propensity to consume (MPC) is increased
    (E) none of the above

119. The most important function of the Federal Reserve System is
    (A) controlling the money supply
    (B) issuing currency
    (C) lending money to commercial banks
    (D) overseeing the transactions between commercial banks and consumers
    (E) informing the U.S. government of fluctuations in the money supply

120. Currency and checkable deposits held by the Federal Reserve and U.S. government
    (A) are backed by its equal value of gold and silver
    (B) help decrease the rate of inflation
    (C) inadvertently increase the rate of inflation
    (D) may only be counted as a store of value
    (E) are not included in the M1 money supply

121. If a loan is repaid at a commercial bank
    (A) money is destroyed
    (B) money is created
    (C) commercial bank assets are increased
    (D) commercial bank assets are decreased
    (E) none of the above

122. If interest rates increase, there will be
    (A) an increase in the demand for money
    (B) a decrease in the total amount of money demanded
    (C) an increase in the total amount of money demanded
    (D) a decrease in the total amount of money supplied
    (E) an increase in the frequency of loans given at commercial banks

123. Members of the Federal Reserve Board of Governors are rarely subject to political pressure because
    (A) they are appointed by the president to 14-year terms
    (B) they are selected by the Federal Open Market Committee to 14-year terms
    (C) they are selected by each of the Federal Reserve banks
    (D) they are appointed by the U.S. Congress to 14-year terms
    (E) it is their job not to be swayed by politics

124. If the required reserve ratio is 25% and a commercial bank has $2 million in cash, $1 million in government securities, $3 million on deposit at a Federal Reserve bank, and $6 million in demand deposits, its total reserves are
    (A) $3 million
    (B) $4 million
    (C) $5 million
    (D) $8 million
    (E) $12 million

125. If Leo deposits $150 in his checking account and later that day Leo's friend Terri negotiates a loan for $5,000 at the same bank, how will this affect the supply of money?

(A) Increased by $5,000
(B) Decreased by $5,000
(C) Increased by $4,850
(D) Decreased by $4,850
(E) No change in the money supply

126. Two conflicting goals of a commercial bank are

(A) buying and selling government securities
(B) buying government securities and its liabilities
(C) liquidity and profits
(D) savings and checking
(E) selling government securities and its liabilities

127. A valid reason for requiring commercial banks to have reserve requirements is to

(A) ensure the banks have money for loans
(B) ensure the banks have enough money for withdrawals
(C) provide a system in which the transactions of banks may be monitored and controlled
(D) provide a system in which banks are held accountable for their transactions
(E) all of the above

128. Varying the money supply in a economy is beneficial because

(A) it will help during fluctuations in the business cycle
(B) it will push consumers to use currency over checkable deposits
(C) it will decrease inflation
(D) it will increase inflation
(E) it will decrease unemployment

129. M1 money supply refers to

(A) time accounts
(B) currency and credit card accounts
(C) coins and paper money held by the public
(D) savings deposits and money market deposit accounts
(E) all of the above

130. M2 money supply refers to

    (A) M1 money, savings accounts, and other time deposits
    (B) savings accounts only
    (C) time deposits only
    (D) M1 money subtracted from M3 money
    (E) none of the above

Use the following graph to answer questions 131 and 132. This graph depicts the supply of money in an economy.

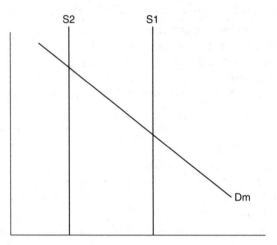

131. The shift from S1 to S2 on the preceding money supply graph was most likely caused by

    (A) the Federal Reserve selling government securities on the open market
    (B) the Federal Reserve buying government securities on the open market
    (C) the Federal Reserve decreasing the discount rate
    (D) the Federal Reserve lowering the reserve ratio
    (E) an increase in government spending

132. The shift from S1 to S2 on the preceding money supply graph was possibly an attempt to

    (A) decrease output of productivity
    (B) decrease the current account surplus
    (C) decrease inflation
    (D) increase the price level
    (E) stimulate the economy out of a recession

133. Which of the following reflects the two components of the demand for money?
    (A) Stocks and bonds
    (B) Checkable deposits and savings accounts
    (C) Buying and selling of government securities
    (D) Transactions demand and asset demand
    (E) All of the above

134. A stock is
    (A) a claim of ownership in a business
    (B) a certificate of indebtedness
    (C) traded in a closed market system
    (D) a guarantee of future prices to be traded on the stock market
    (E) all of the above

135. A bond is
    (A) used if a business wants to raise money by borrowing money to be repaid plus a specific rate of interest
    (B) a claim of ownership in a business
    (C) not traded on the stock market
    (D) rarely used in a free market system
    (E) all of the above

136. The best explanation of the quantity theory of money would be
    (A) that it measures the maximum amount of new checking deposits that can be created by a single dollar in excess reserves
    (B) the interest rate paid on short-term loans
    (C) nominal GDP is equal to the quantity of money
    (D) the average number of times a dollar is spent in a year
    (E) the amount of money determines the price level

137. What is one effect an increase in the money supply will have on the economy?
    (A) It will raise the price level and have no effect on real GDP.
    (B) It will raise the price level and have an effect on real GDP.
    (C) It will lower the price level and have no effect on real GDP.
    (D) It will lower the price level and have an effect on real GDP.
    (E) It will raise the price level and affect nominal GDP.

138. What is a usual course of action if a firm desires to raise investment funds?

(A) Debt financing
(B) Increasing its liquid assets
(C) Decreasing its liquid assets
(D) Increasing transaction demand
(E) Increasing asset demand

139. If Jack deposits $500, and the reserve ratio is 10%, what will result?

(A) $5,000 in money creation
(B) $5,000 in money destruction
(C) $500 in money creation
(D) $550 in money destruction
(E) $50 in money creation

Use the following scenario to answer questions 140 and 141: Jennifer and Christopher are out shopping at their local mall. They walk pass a storefront window and see a sign that states, "Electronic back scratchers $50!"

140. In this scenario, money is serving which purpose?

(A) Store of value
(B) Unit of account
(C) Medium of exchange
(D) Checkable deposit
(E) None of the above

141. Christopher decides to buy the electronic back scratcher. He brings it up to the counter and hands the cashier the money to purchase the product. In this scenario, money is serving as

(A) a store of value
(B) a unit of account
(C) a checkable deposit
(D) M1 money
(E) a medium of exchange

142. All of the following are ways the Federal Reserve can change the money supply EXCEPT

(A) buying government securities
(B) selling government securities
(C) changing current tax rates
(D) changing the reserve ratio
(E) changing the discount rate

143. All of the following are assets held by Bank XYZ EXCEPT

    (A) money on reserve

    (B) loans made to businesses

    (C) cash withdrawals

    (D) loans made out to citizens

    (E) a home mortgage

144. Something that is used as money but also has intrinsic value in some other use is known as

    (A) barter money

    (B) commodity money

    (C) a medium of exchange

    (D) a store of value

    (E) a unit of account

145. The Federal Reserve System is

    (A) responsible for establishing monetary and fiscal policy

    (B) responsible for establishing fiscal policy only

    (C) the central bank of the United States

    (D) only allowed to set interest rates

    (E) only allowed to buy government securities

146. Currency in your wallet, travelers' checks, and checkable deposits represent

    (A) M1 money supply

    (B) M2 money supply

    (C) M3 money supply

    (D) M1 and M2 money supply

    (E) M1 and M3 money supply

147. If the Federal Reserve lowered the reserve ratio to 5%, what would be the money multiplier?

    (A) 20

    (B) 10

    (C) 5

    (D) 50

    (E) 25

148. All of the following will increase the money supply EXCEPT

(A) the Federal Reserve buying government securities
(B) the Federal Reserve decreasing the reserve ratio
(C) the Federal Reserve increasing the reserve ratio
(D) a decrease in the discount rate
(E) a decrease in taxes

149. The value of a bond will decrease if

(A) interest rates increase
(B) interest rates decrease
(C) a person does not cash the bond when it matures
(D) the Federal Reserve decides to sell government securities
(E) the Federal Reserve decides to buy government securities

150. A bank's biggest liability is

(A) mortgages
(B) investments in a money market
(C) bonds
(D) stocks
(E) checkable deposits

CHAPTER 9

Inflation, Unemployment, and Stabilization Policies

151. Changes made to fiscal policy would involve changes in

    (A) interest rates

    (B) the reserve ratio

    (C) the discount rate

    (D) the U.S. constitution

    (E) taxation and government spending

152. Which of the following illustrates a contractionary fiscal policy?

    (A) An increase in taxation and a decrease in government spending

    (B) An increase in taxation and an increase in government spending

    (C) A decrease in taxation and a decrease in government spending

    (D) No change in taxation and an increase in government spending

    (E) An increase in taxation and no change in government spending

153. Decreasing government spending while increasing the tax rate would be the best policy for combating

    (A) a recession

    (B) inflation

    (C) structural unemployment

    (D) an expansionary fiscal policy

    (E) a decreasing average price level

154. The U.S. Congress lowered taxes to aid in the recovery from a recession. This is an example of

    (A) the political business cycle

    (B) contractionary fiscal policy

    (C) discretionary fiscal policy

    (D) nondiscretionary fiscal policy

    (E) expansionary monetary policy

155. A decrease in aggregate demand would be implemented by

(A) a contractionary fiscal policy
(B) no change in the price level
(C) an increase in aggregate supply
(D) a decrease in aggregate supply
(E) an expansionary fiscal policy

156. A set of fiscal policies that would counteract each other would be

(A) a decrease in government spending and no change in taxes
(B) an increase in government spending and an increase in taxes
(C) a decrease in government spending and a decrease in taxes
(D) a decrease in government spending and buying government securities
(E) an increase in government spending and selling government securities

Use the following diagram to answer questions 157 and 158.

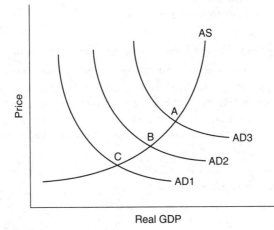

157. According to the preceding diagram, the economy is at equilibrium at Point A. Choose the best fiscal policy most appropriate to control demand-pull inflation.

(A) Decrease aggregate demand by increasing taxes
(B) Increase aggregate demand by decreasing taxes
(C) Decrease aggregate supply by increasing taxes
(D) Increase aggregate demand by increasing government spending
(E) Decrease aggregate supply by selling government securities

158. According to the preceding diagram, the economy is at equilibrium at Point B. Choose the best fiscal policy that would increase real GDP.

  (A) Increase aggregate demand from AD2 to AD1 by decreasing taxes
  (B) Decrease aggregate demand from AD2 toAD3 by increasing government spending
  (C) Decrease aggregate demand from AD2 to AD3 by decreasing government spending
  (D) Increase aggregate demand from AD2 to AD3 by decreasing taxes
  (E) Increase aggregate demand from AD2 to AD3 by buying government securities

159. Imagine the economy is in a recession. Which of the following fiscal policy suggestions would most likely be recommended?

  (A) Increase government spending or increase taxation
  (B) Increase government spending and decrease taxation
  (C) Increase government spending and increase taxation
  (D) Decrease government spending and decrease taxation
  (E) A and B

160. If the U.S. government wanted to increase aggregate demand by $50 billion and the MPS is 0.4, then it should

  (A) increase government spending by $20 billion
  (B) increase government spending by $10 billion
  (C) decrease government spending by $20 billion
  (D) decrease government spending by $10 billion
  (E) increase taxes by $20 billion

161. The crowding out effect may be avoided if

  (A) the government pursues a contractionary fiscal policy
  (B) aggregate demand is increased
  (C) the government destroys a percentage of the money supply
  (D) the government issues new money
  (E) A and D

162. If the United States is experiencing a deficit, and a course of action is to issue new money,

  (A) the crowding out effect may be avoided
  (B) the crowding out effect is unavoidable
  (C) interest rates will increase
  (D) interest rates will decrease
  (E) none of the above

163. Due to automatic stabilizers, if income increases, government transfer spending
    (A) increases and tax revenues decrease
    (B) stays the same and tax revenues decrease
    (C) stays the same and tax revenues increase
    (D) decreases
    (E) none of the above

164. What is often a result of full employment?
    (A) The rate of inflation is zero.
    (B) The MPS is 1.
    (C) The MPC is 1.
    (D) There is a balanced budget.
    (E) Inflation increases.

165. The crowding out effect refers to which of the following?
    (A) Increases in government spending may raise the interest rate and reduce investment.
    (B) Increases in government spending will shorten the recessionary gap.
    (C) Decreases in consumption will increase taxes.
    (D) High taxes reduce savings and decrease investment.
    (E) High taxes increase savings and increase investment.

166. If the U.S. government adopts a fiscal policy that is
    (A) expansionary, then net exports will likely increase
    (B) expansionary, then net exports will likely decrease
    (C) contractionary, then government securities will likely decrease
    (D) contractionary, then government securities will likely increase
    (E) none of the above

167. As a result of a progressive tax system, as income increases, the average tax rate will
    (A) increase
    (B) decrease
    (C) increase at first and then gradually level off
    (D) decrease at first and then gradually level off
    (E) remain the same

168. Which fiscal policy would be the most contractionary?

    (A) a $100 billion decrease in government spending

    (B) a $100 billion increase in government spending

    (C) a $90 billion decrease in government spending and a $10 billion decrease in taxes

    (D) a $90 increase in government spending

    (E) none of the above

169. Suppose the U.S. economy is at potential GDP. If there is an increase in the money supply

    (A) hyperinflation will result

    (B) stagflation will result

    (C) depreciation will result

    (D) demand-pull inflation will result

    (E) cost-push inflation will result

170. Cost-push inflation will occur if

    (A) government regulation is decreased

    (B) government spending is increased

    (C) producers increase wages without gains in output

    (D) there is an increase in investment spending

    (E) B, C, and D

171. What happens to the Phillips curve in the long run?

    (A) It will become vertical.

    (B) It will become horizontal intersecting the long-run aggregate supply curve.

    (C) It will run parallel to the Laffer curve.

    (D) It will run parallel to the short-run aggregate supply curve.

    (E) A, C, and D

172. Both monetary and fiscal policy will have zero effect on real GDP

    (A) when the aggregate supply curve is in the long run

    (B) when the aggregate supply curve is in the short run

    (C) when contractionary policies are enacted by the Federal Reserve

    (D) when expansionary policies are enacted by the Federal Reserve

    (E) when expansionary policies are enacted by the Federal Reserve and contractionary fiscal policies are enacted by the U.S. government

173. A recession is likely to occur if

(A) there is an increase in real GDP over a long period of time
(B) there is an increase in real GDP over a two-year period of time
(C) the government does not respond to demand-pull inflation with policy actions
(D) GDP falls for two consecutive quarters
(E) price levels remain constant and do not adjust to nominal GDP

174. If there is an increase in the money supply, then it was caused by

(A) a decrease in the money supply
(B) the Federal Reserve Bank
(C) the federal government
(D) a contractionary fiscal policy
(E) none of the above

175. Mike is watching the news and hears the broadcaster say, "The government will begin to monetize the deficit." Curious about this statement, Mike asks his friend, who is an AP Economics teacher, about it. His friend explains that this statement means

(A) the Federal Reserve will print more money, which may result in inflation
(B) the Federal Reserve will print more money, which will decrease inflation
(C) the Federal Reserve will sell more government securities
(D) the Treasury will begin to repay the deficit
(E) the U.S. Congress will ask the Federal Reserve to increase the interest rate

176. Which of the following would be a contractionary monetary policy?

(A) Selling government securities
(B) Buying government securities
(C) Increasing spending on government projects
(D) Increasing income taxes
(E) Decreasing income taxes

177. What is a benefit of expansionary monetary policy?

(A) Aggregate demand will increase, but employment will decrease.
(B) Aggregate demand will decrease, but employment will increase.
(C) Aggregate demand will increase, and employment will increase.
(D) Aggregate supply will increase, and employment will increase.
(E) None of the above

178. Suppose the Federal Reserve increases the money supply and investment spending increases by $10 billion. What will happen to the aggregate demand if the MPC is 0.7?

(A) Increase by $33 billion
(B) Increase by $14 billion
(C) Decrease by $14 billion
(D) Decrease by $3 billion
(E) Increase by $3 billion

179. One advantage of monetary policy over fiscal policy is

(A) the speed at which it can be implemented
(B) the regulation of taxes and government spending
(C) the slow, methodical, and thoughtful pace at which it can be implemented
(D) its effectiveness on aggregate supply over aggregate demand
(E) A and B

180. The lending power of commercial banks decreases when

(A) central banks buy securities in the open market
(B) central banks sell securities in the open market
(C) the reserve ratio is decreased
(D) the U.S. Treasury collects increased income tax
(E) the Federal Reserve lowers the interest rate

181. If the Federal Reserve decided to pursue a contractionary policy, which actions would tend to offset each other?

(A) Selling government securities and lowering the discount rate
(B) Selling government securities and raising the discount rate
(C) Buying government securities and lowering the discount rate
(D) Buying government securities and raising the discount rate
(E) Buying government securities and lowering the reserve ratio

182. Imagine the economy is experiencing high unemployment and a low rate of economic growth. What policy should the Federal Reserve follow?

(A) Pursue an easy money policy and sell government securities
(B) Pursue a tight money policy and sell government securities
(C) Pursue a tight money policy and buy government securities
(D) Pursue an easy money policy and raise the reserve ratio
(E) Pursue an easy money policy and buy government securities

183. What happens to the money supply if the Federal Reserve pursues a tight money policy?

(A) Increases
(B) Decreases
(C) Remains the same
(D) Equals full employment
(E) None of the above

184. Suppose you read a *Wall Street Journal* article that states the Federal Reserve will lower the discount rate for the third time this year. According to this article, the Federal Reserve is trying to

(A) reduce inflation
(B) increase inflation
(C) stimulate the economy
(D) aid the U.S. Treasury
(E) increase checkable deposits

185. Suppose the economy is experiencing stable prices but high unemployment. Which monetary and fiscal policies would help reduce unemployment?

(A) Purchase government securities and increase government spending
(B) Purchase government securities and decrease government spending
(C) Sell government securities and decrease government spending
(D) Sell government securities and increase government spending
(E) Purchase government securities and increase taxes

186. If the Federal Reserve buys $50 million in government securities, then the money supply will

(A) decrease by $50 million
(B) increase by $25 million
(C) increase by $50 million
(D) increase by $25 million and the purchasing power of commercial banks will increase by $25 million
(E) none of the above

187. One disadvantage of monetary policy is

(A) the speed at which it can be implemented
(B) difficulty with breaking inflation
(C) isolation from political pressure
(D) reduction of trade deficits
(E) the velocity of money

188. For the Federal Reserve, the largest asset is

(A) securities
(B) loans to commercial banks
(C) Federal Reserve notes
(D) deposits from the U.S. Treasury
(E) all of the above

189. The main purpose of an easy money policy is to

(A) decrease aggregate demand
(B) increase aggregate demand
(C) increase aggregate supply
(D) decrease aggregate supply
(E) increase investment spending

190. Demand-pull inflation refers to

(A) aggregate demand moving at a quicker pace than aggregate supply, thus an increase in price
(B) aggregate demand moving at a slower pace than aggregate supply, thus an increase in price
(C) an increase in prices brought on by a discovery of a new resource or new technology
(D) an increase in the price level from an increase in the cost of production
(E) the high cost of production being pushed onto the consumer

Use the following graph to answer question 191.

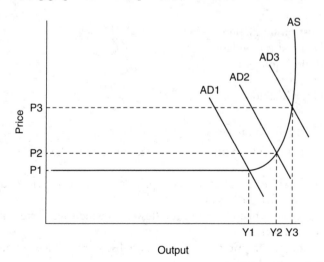

191. According to the preceding graph, which type of inflation would most likely occur?

(A) Cost-push inflation
(B) Built-in inflation
(C) Demand-pull inflation
(D) Stagflation
(E) Hyperinflation

Use the following graph to answer question 192.

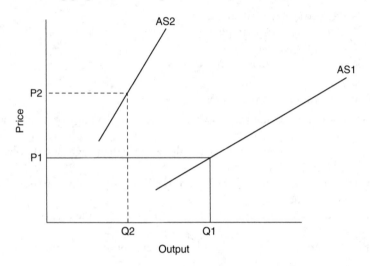

192. According to the preceding graph, what type of inflation would most likely occur?

(A) Cost-push inflation
(B) Demand-pull inflation
(C) Built-in inflation
(D) Stagflation
(E) Hyperinflation

193. Cost-push inflation refers to

(A) an increase in the price level from an increase in the cost of production
(B) aggregate demand moving at a quicker pace than aggregate supply, thus an increase in price
(C) aggregate demand moving at a slower pace than aggregate supply, thus an increase in price
(D) an increase in prices brought on by a discovery of a new resource or new technology
(E) the increase in the price level due to hyperinflation

194. _____ fiscal policy tries to solve the problem of recession, whereas _____ fiscal policy tries to solve the problem of inflation.

(A) Expansionary, contractionary
(B) Contractionary, expansionary
(C) Tight, easy
(D) Expansionary, expansionary
(E) Contractionary, contractionary

195. The main purpose of a built-in stabilizer is to

(A) increase the government surplus during a recession without changing policy
(B) increase or decrease the government surplus without changing policy
(C) decrease the government surplus during inflation without changing policy
(D) increase or decrease the government surplus with a fast-pace change in policy
(E) bring the economy to full employment without changing policy

196. Built-in stabilizers are a part of

(A) discretionary fiscal policy
(B) discretionary monetary policy
(C) nondiscretionary monetary policy
(D) nondiscretionary fiscal policy
(E) balancing net imports and exports

197. A major problem or concern with fiscal policy is

(A) recognition lag
(B) inflation
(C) stagflation
(D) the swift pace at which it is implemented
(E) all of the above

198. Which of the following would be an advantage of automatic stabilizers?

(A) No additional policy or legislation is needed.
(B) They are more influential than discretionary fiscal policy.
(C) They always increase aggregate demand.
(D) They always increase aggregate supply.
(E) A and C

199. The Organization of Petroleum Exporting Countries (OPEC) dramatically increased the price of crude oil in 1973. The price of gasoline in the United States and around the world increased. This increase in price was

  (A) hyperinflation
  (B) stagflation
  (C) demand-pull inflation
  (D) cost-push inflation
  (E) none of the above

200. The main tools of the Federal Reserve are

  (A) buying/selling securities, the discount rate, and increasing/decreasing taxes
  (B) buying/selling securities, the reserve ratio, and increasing/decreasing taxes
  (C) buying/selling securities, the discount rate, and the reserve ratio
  (D) the discount rate, the reserve ratio, and increasing/decreasing taxes
  (E) buying government securities, the discount rate, and the reserve ratio

201. If the Federal Reserve decided to increase the discount rate, then it would be

  (A) following a tight money policy
  (B) following an easy money policy
  (C) trying to sell government securities
  (D) trying to buy government securities
  (E) forcing commercial banks to increase the amount of money they must keep in reserve

202. Suppose there is a leftward shift in aggregate demand due to an increase in interest rates as a result of expansionary fiscal policy. This is known as

  (A) the crowding out effect
  (B) an inflationary gap
  (C) a recessionary gap
  (D) cost-push inflation
  (E) demand-pull inflation

203. If the Federal Reserve decreases the discount rate,

  (A) it will be more difficult for commercial banks to borrow money
  (B) it will contract the economy
  (C) it will be easier for commercial banks to borrow money
  (D) it is attempting to decrease inflation
  (E) it is attempting to combat demand-pull inflation

204. If the Federal Reserve decided to lower the required reserve ratio, then this would

(A) contract the economy
(B) raise the price level
(C) lower the price level
(D) expand the economy
(E) decrease deposits

205. The average number of times per year a dollar is spent is known as

(A) the quantity theory of money
(B) cost-push inflation
(C) the velocity of money
(D) the capital account
(E) the rate of inflation

CHAPTER 10

Economic Growth and Productivity

206. An increase in per capita GDP

  (A) leads to an increase in the standard of living
  (B) leads to a decrease in the standard of living
  (C) leads to contractionary measures taken by the Federal Reserve
  (D) leads to a decrease in consumer investment
  (E) leads to a decrease in the labor force

207. If the U.S. economy has a 2% annual growth rate, how long will it take for real GDP to double?

  (A) 140 years
  (B) 35 years
  (C) 40 years
  (D) 17.5 years
  (E) 70 years

208. All of the following influence a nation's rate of growth EXCEPT

  (A) capital stocks
  (B) skill level of the labor force
  (C) growth of the labor force
  (D) growth of technology
  (E) an increasing inflation rate

209. Allocative efficiency refers to

  (A) utilizing resources to produce goods and services that maximize a society's benefit
  (B) utilizing resources to produce goods and services in the cheapest way possible
  (C) measuring the gross domestic product to assess the time it will take to double
  (D) increasing the productivity of goods and services
  (E) maximizing output of goods and services to beyond the production possibilities frontier

210. The Rule of 70 refers to
    (A) calculating the inflation rate
    (B) estimating how long scarce natural resources will last
    (C) measuring economic growth through the gross domestic product
    (D) measuring domestic output
    (E) measuring domestic output against foreign imports

211. GDP per capita refers to
    (A) nominal GDP
    (B) real GDP
    (C) GNP
    (D) GDP adjusted in inflationary terms
    (E) GDP calculated per person

212. If an economy increased its output without utilizing an increase in the factors of production, it is said that
    (A) technological progress occurred
    (B) there was an increase in the labor force
    (C) foreign imports decreased for that year
    (D) more businesses used more capital but less labor
    (E) more businesses used less capital but more labor

213. Economists calculate how wealthy nations are by measuring their
    (A) GNP
    (B) debt to GDP ratio
    (C) GDP
    (D) inflation rate
    (E) GDP per capita

214. Derek works as a construction worker. Recently, he became certified to operate a large construction crane used to build skyscrapers. Economists would refer to this knowledge and skill as
    (A) capital
    (B) a scarce resource
    (C) human capital
    (D) capital stock
    (E) technological progress

215. If there is an increase in capital stock, it will most likely lead to

(A) an increase in GDP and wages
(B) a decrease in GDP but not wages
(C) a decrease in GDP and wages
(D) an increase in wages but not GDP
(E) no change in GDP and wages

216. Suppose there is a major increase in population after five years. This will most likely result in

(A) a decrease in GDP per capita and an increase in real GDP
(B) a decrease in GDP per capita and a decrease in real GDP
(C) an increase in GDP per capita and a decrease in real GDP
(D) an increase in GDP per capita and an increase in real GDP
(E) no change in GDP per capita and real GDP

217. The president of the United States encourages Americans to help the economy grow. One suggestion would most likely be to

(A) buy imported goods
(B) increase consumption
(C) support relaxed immigration laws to increase the population
(D) save and invest
(E) accumulate wealth

CHAPTER 11

International Trade and Finance

218. Some predictable outcomes of an import quota on foreign motorbikes for consumers and domestic producers are

   I. higher prices for consumers
  II. lower prices for consumers
 III. protection for domestic producers
 IV. an increase in domestic efficiency

(A) I only
(B) I and III only
(C) I, II, IV only
(D) III and IV only
(E) IV only

219. Which of the following best describes the capital account on a nation's balance of payments?

(A) The current export payments of goods and services
(B) A limited amount of foreign currency
(C) The purchase of foreign real estate assets
(D) The sale of domestic real estate and financial assets
(E) The purchase and sale of real and financial assets between nations

220. China's economy is enjoying growth and expansion. How will this affect U.S. net exports, the value of the dollar, and the Chinese yuan?

	U.S. Net Exports	Value of Dollar	Value of Yuan
(A)	Decrease	Increase	Increase
(B)	Increase	Decrease	Increase
(C)	Decrease	Decrease	Increase
(D)	Increase	Increase	Increase
(E)	Increase	Increase	Decrease

221. When U.S. interests rates rise, we see

    I. an increase in capital investment
    II. foreign tastes for American goods strengthen
    III. a decrease in capital investments and an increase in financial investments
    IV. a decrease in financial investments

    (A) I and IV only
    (B) III only
    (C) I, II, and II only
    (D) II only
    (E) III and IV only

222. A tariff refers to

    (A) a prohibition against trading particular goods
    (B) an elimination of trade with foreign nations
    (C) the restriction on the sale of exports in another country
    (D) a tax on imported goods
    (E) the price difference between production cost and sale price

223. In a competitive market, nation XYZ produces bananas. Assuming there is free trade and the domestic price is higher than the world price, which of the following is true?

    (A) There are no benefits to importing or exporting bananas.
    (B) Nation XYZ will import bananas to eliminate a domestic surplus.
    (C) Nation XYZ will export bananas to correct a domestic shortage.
    (D) Nation XYZ will import bananas to correct a domestic shortage.
    (E) Nation XYZ will export bananas to eliminate a domestic surplus.

224. Suppose the United States has a surplus balance in the current account. Which of the following statements is true?

    (A) There is a balance of payments deficit.
    (B) There was more foreign capital invested in the United States than there was U.S. investment abroad.
    (C) There is a trade surplus.
    (D) The United States sent more dollars abroad than there was foreign currency received.
    (E) There is a trade deficit.

225. When the United States places an import quota on imported rice,

  (A) consumers will buy rice substitutes
  (B) consumers will use more rice and rice products
  (C) the supply of rice decreases
  (D) the United States will begin to export less rice
  (E) makers of U.S. rice products suffer

226. Which of the following is a benefit of a protective tariff on imported timber?

  (A) The domestic timber industry is made vulnerable to global competition.
  (B) The domestic timber industry is protected from global competition.
  (C) The price of foreign timber decreases.
  (D) The United States consumes more foreign timber.
  (E) There are no known benefits of a protective tariff.

227. The United States instates a protective tariff on particular goods to

  (A) limit the amount of goods imported into the country
  (B) increase the amount of goods imported into the country
  (C) encourage trade with foreign competitors
  (D) protect itself from foreign competition
  (E) balance a trade deficit

228. Tariffs and quotas share many of the same economic effects. Which of the following statements is false?

  (A) Economic resources are reallocated toward inefficient producers.
  (B) Lower consumer surpluses hurt consumers.
  (C) Artificially high prices hurt consumers.
  (D) Inefficient domestic producers are protected at the expense of foreign firms creating dead weight loss.
  (E) Tariffs and quotas collect revenue for the government.

229. If the U.S. dollar depreciates relative to the Chinese yuan, then

  (A) U.S. goods sold in China would become cheaper
  (B) U.S. goods sold in China would become more expensive
  (C) more yuan are needed to buy a dollar
  (D) prices would not differ for U.S. or Chinese goods
  (E) none of the above

230. When the Japanese yen decreases in value relative to another currency, it has
    (A) appreciated
    (B) depreciated
    (C) fixed
    (D) floated
    (E) inflated

231. Honda buys an automobile factory in Ohio. On the U.S. balance of payments this is recorded
    (A) as outflow on U.S. assets abroad
    (B) on the Official Reserves on the U.S. balance of payments
    (C) as net investment income
    (D) in the current account
    (E) in the capital account as inflow of foreign assets to the United States

232. The law of comparative advantage states
    (A) the more a nation produces of any one good, production costs rise
    (B) the more a nation produces of any one good, production costs fall
    (C) nations can mutually benefit from trade as long as the relative production costs differ
    (D) all nations benefit from international trade
    (E) all nations benefit from free trade

233. According to the theory of comparative advantage, a nation should
    (A) produce and export goods that have low labor costs
    (B) produce and export goods that have low monetary costs
    (C) produce and export goods that have high labor costs
    (D) produce and export goods that have low opportunity costs
    (E) produce and export goods that have high opportunity costs

234. Floating exchange rates are determined by
    (A) unregulated forces of supply and demand
    (B) the Federal Reserve
    (C) fiscal policy
    (D) the balance between exports and imports
    (E) protective tariffs

235. The sum of the current account and the capital account is known as

(A) the balance of payments
(B) the foreign exchange rate
(C) the floating exchange rate
(D) the fixed exchange rate
(E) the rate of inflation

236. If the U.S. dollar increases in value as compared to a foreign currency, it is said that the U.S. dollar

(A) depreciated
(B) expanded
(C) shifted in value
(D) appreciated
(E) floated

237. If the U.S. dollar decreases in value as compared to a foreign currency, it is said that the U.S. dollar

(A) depreciated
(B) expanded
(C) shifted in value
(D) appreciated
(E) floated

238. Which act of Congress increased the severity of the Great Depression of the 1930s?

(A) The Smoot-Hawley Act
(B) Economic Opportunity Act
(C) The New Deal
(D) NAFT(A)
(E) The Davis-Bacon Act

239. The United States will have a trade surplus if

(A) the value of commodity exports exceeds the value of commodity imports
(B) the value of commodity imports exceeds the value of commodity imports
(C) there is a fixed exchange rate established by U.S. Congress and not the market forces of supply and demand
(D) the market forces of supply and demand are allowed to set the exchange rate between two nations
(E) the U.S. dollar appreciates compared to a foreign currency

240. If foreign currency being sent to the United States exceeds the dollars being sent out, it is said that the United States has a

(A) positive current account
(B) negative capital account
(C) positive capital account
(D) negative current account
(E) trade deficit

241. The difference between domestic price and world price is

(A) world prices are established above the equilibrium price
(B) domestic prices are usually below the world price equilibrium point
(C) domestic prices are used within a nation, and world prices are used between nations engaged in trade
(D) revenue tariffs are higher when nations engage in world prices
(E) revenue tariffs are lower when nations engage in world prices

242. The capital account refers to

(A) protective tariffs
(B) import quotas
(C) balance of payment
(D) the flow of investments between domestic and foreign nations
(E) the global equilibrium price of a good

243. Consumer tastes and relative income are

(A) factors that determine the exchange rate
(B) factors that determine the capital account
(C) factors that determine world prices
(D) factors that determine the equilibrium between supply and demand
(E) all of the above

244. An increase in aggregate supply may result in

(A) an increase in the foreign exchange value of a country's currency
(B) a decrease in the foreign exchange value of a country's currency
(C) an increase in a nation's net exports
(D) a decrease in a nation's net exports
(E) none of the above

245. The appreciation of a nation's currency relative to foreign currencies will

(A) increase that nation's exports

(B) decrease that nation's exports

(C) decrease that nation's exports and imports

(D) decrease tariffs

(E) increase the foreign exchange rate

246. A major argument for the North American free-trade zone was

(A) it would increase the loss of American jobs

(B) the United States, Canada, and Mexico would specialize according to comparative advantage

(C) the United States, Canada, and Mexico would not specialize according to comparative advantage

(D) North American nations wanted to compete with the European Union

(E) it would increase North American exports

247. One major example of economic integration in the Western Hemisphere in recent years is

(A) the European Union

(B) the World Trade Organization

(C) the North American Free Trade Agreement

(D) the Smoot-Hawley Act

(E) the Reciprocal Trade Agreements Act

248. A disadvantage of a floating exchange rate is

(A) trade may worsen due to a nation's depreciation of its currency

(B) tariffs cease to be effective

(C) exports decrease

(D) imports decrease

(E) all of the above

249. A strong dollar hurts

(A) an Englishman traveling to America

(B) an American traveling to a foreign country

(C) businesses that import foreign goods

(D) the fixed exchange rate

(E) competition among foreign competitors

250. A strong dollar helps

- (A) an American traveling to a foreign country
- (B) businesses that export goods
- (C) the foreign exchange rate
- (D) competition among foreign competitors
- (E) the strength of the European Union

ANSWERS

Chapter 5: Basic Economic Concepts

1. (A) This is the best choice for a definition of macroeconomics. Macroeconomics looks at the big picture; gross domestic product, unemployment, and inflation all relate to economics on a national or global scale. Choice B is incorrect because it is a very general and basic understanding of economics. Choice C is incorrect because this fits on a smaller scale, which a person studying microeconomics would like to know. Choice D is incorrect because it deals with facts versus value judgments.

2. (A) This is the best answer because Line A represents a supply curve, which is upward sloping. Choices B, C, and D are incorrect because they are downward sloping, which indicates a demand curve.

3. (B) In any choice people make, they must look at the relationship between marginal benefit and marginal cost. If a decision, whether it be purchasing an item or going for a walk, costs more than the benefit, then the person should not do it. Choice A is incorrect because we do not know the next best decision to buying the Xbox, which would indicate the opportunity cost.

4. (A) The key to understanding comparative advantage is to understand opportunity cost. If a producer can make a good at a lower opportunity cost than all other producers, it is said that the producer has a comparative advantage. Choices B, C, and D do not incorporate opportunity cost; therefore, they are incorrect.

5. (D) You must know the differences between micro- and macroeconomics to answer this question. Choice D is the best answer because issues like price inflation, imports, and labor represent economics on a large scale. Choices A, C, and E represent microeconomic issues because they involve individual markets. Choice B is incorrect because this determinant for demand is true for both micro- and macroeconomics.

6. (E) Trade will exist between two countries if there is a comparative advantage between the two countries or each country is producing its good at a lower opportunity cost than the other. Choice A would certainly be good for both countries, but the question asks when it is truly beneficial for two countries to trade with each other. Choice B is incorrect because it refers to a decrease in production costs as output increases, which does not factor into trade between two countries. Choice C is the opposite of Choice B and still has nothing to do with trade between two countries. Choice D is incorrect because absolute advantage refers to the ability to produce more of a good than all other producers.

7. (A) The production possibilities curve represents the maximum output between two goods. It also reflects the opportunity costs between these two goods because resources are scarce. Any point along the curve is the maximum output producing both of the goods and therefore is an attainable and efficient use of resources. Choices B and C do not reflect this maximum output. Choice D is incorrect because this would be represented by a point inside the production possibilities curve, not on it.

8. (A) This is the best answer because in economics, "growth" is always represented by a rightward movement of any curve on any graph. Choices B and C are incorrect because they reflect movement along the curve, not the movement of the curve itself. Choice D is incorrect because the intersection of the supply and demand curves is the equilibrium point where price is usually set. Choice E is incorrect because it is unrelated to economic growth.

9. (C) The production possibilities curve represents the maximum output between two goods using scarce resources. As such, it represents the opportunity costs incurred when the production shifts to more of one product than the other. The more a producer chooses to make of a product, the more the opportunity costs increase for the product not being produced. Choice A is incorrect because it reflects the opposite idea of a production possibilities curve. Choice B is incorrect because a production possibilities curve reflects only the production combination of two goods, not taxes.

10. (A) Choice A is the best answer because an opportunity cost is the most profitable alternative given up when you make a decision; Tommy could have earned $20 tutoring his brother for two hours. Choices B and C are incorrect because the question does not ask for the marginal benefits and marginal costs. Choice D is incorrect because Tommy is giving up the chance to earn $20, so it would never be an opportunity cost of zero.

11. (C) This is the best choice because it best represents the concept of opportunity cost. Choices A and B are incorrect because they represent only the costs incurred while building the performing arts center, not the next best alternative.

12. (A) Discovery of a new resource is a fundamental factor that results in economic growth. Economic growth is represented by a rightward shift of the production possibilities curve. Since Tanen found the resource, it would affect only its curve and not Reilly's. Choices C and D are incorrect because a leftward shift indicates a contracting economy.

13. (D) If a society overallocates its resources, then it is acting excessively. In any economic decision, it is always best to have marginal benefit greater than marginal cost. But if resources are being spread too thin, then marginal cost is usually greater than marginal benefit.

14. (B) Government ownership of the factors of production exists under a command economy, not in a market economy. A market economy is based on the freedom of the market forces of supply and demand.

15. (E) The production possibilities curve represents the maximum output between two goods using scarce resources. Choice A represents the relationship between tax rates and government revenue. Choice B represents the relationship between inflation and unemployment. Choice C is incorrect because the equilibrium point represents the price level. Choice D is incorrect because it represents where marginal costs increase as one additional unit of product is produced.

16. (E) In micro- and macroeconomics, the idea of scarcity always juxtaposes human beings' unlimited wants with limited natural resources. Choice E is the best answer. All other choices do not reflect this relationship.

17. (C) Choice C is the best answer because it best reflects the idea of comparative advantage. If a producer can make a good at a lower opportunity cost than all the other producers, it is said that he has a comparative advantage. Luca can weed the garden at a lower opportunity cost than Sarah, so it would be mutually beneficial if he weeded the garden and Sarah walked the dog.

18. (C) Choice C is the best answer because any decision would be worth pursuing if the benefits outweigh the costs. Choice A is incorrect because it is an opinion and does not reflect a true economic statement. Choice B is incorrect because if the costs are greater than the benefits, then Joe should not continue training. Choices D and E are both incorrect because opportunity cost refers to the next best alternative, and this scenario does not state an alternative decision.

19. (A) Choice A is the best answer because the difference between supply and aggregate supply is the basic difference between micro- and macroeconomics. Supply is used in microeconomics to represent the total amount of a good available to consumers for an individual market; for example, the supply of apples. Aggregate supply is used in macroeconomics to represent the total supply of all goods in an economy, where the supply level is represented for an entire country.

20. (A) Factors of production are resources that go into producing goods and services. Choice A is correct because these are fundamental resources needed to produce goods and services. Land, labor, and capital are identified as factors of production.

21. (D) An outward shift represents economic growth. The best answer would be an element that is added to the growth of the company. Choice D is the best answer because an increase in skilled workers would increase production. Choices A, B, and C would cause the production possibilities curve to shift to the left.

22. (C) It is translated as "holding other things constant," or "all else equal." This term is used in economics to help describe the effect a variable might have on other economic factors. If other things are not equal, then a variety of factors may change the outcome of an economic decision.

23. (B) Specialization refers to the production of goods based on comparative advantage. If a nation can produce a good at a lower opportunity cost, then it would be beneficial if it specialized in producing that good and traded with another nation that specialized in producing other goods. Obtaining more than the production possibilities curve necessitates specialization and trade. Choices C, D, and E are incorrect because they are factors that shift the production possibilities curve to the right.

24. (A) Choice A is the best answer because it talks about the opportunity cost. The production possibilities curve represents the opportunity cost. Choice B is incorrect because vital resources are always scarce. Choice C is incorrect because that would be a point inside the production possibilities curve. Choice D and E are incorrect because the production possibilities curve does not reflect marginal utility or benefit.

25. (C) In the most general sense, the more a good or service costs, the less people are willing and able to pay for it. This idea is an inverse, or indirect, relationship graphically represented as a downward sloping curve. Choice E is incorrect because it refers to a direct relationship. Choices A and B are incorrect because price will not shift the entire demand curve to the right or the left. Choice D is incorrect because complementary goods are used alongside other goods, like tennis balls and tennis rackets.

26. (A) In a market system, resources are allocated through the decisions of firms and consumers. Price is therefore determined through the equilibrium point between supply and demand. Choice B is incorrect because it reflects the operation of a command economy. Choice C is incorrect because opportunity cost does not influence how prices are determined; rather it is the cost based on the value of the next best alternative. Choice D is incorrect because more information is needed, such as the amount producers are willing to produce at each price level. Choice E is incorrect because the Fed cannot set the price level.

27. (A) Choice A is the best answer because there are very few alternatives or substitutes for cigarettes. As a result, an increase in price would result in no change in demand, making the elasticity of cigarettes inelastic. Choice C is incorrect because there are very few substitutes for cigarettes. Another example would be the elasticity of gasoline; since there are very few substitutes for gasoline and people need to put gas in their cars, there will be very little sensitivity for demand if the price of gasoline increases.

28. (B) Choice B is the best answer because bowling shoes are complementary goods. If a good shows an increase in demand, then all of its complements will show an increase in demand. This is so because if the demand for bowling balls increases, more people are bowling, and therefore, more people will also need bowling shoes.

29. (B) When the market is left to itself without any government regulations, such as price floors or ceilings, the market price is established at the equilibrium point between supply and demand.

30. (A) Remember that macroeconomics studies the economy on a national or global scale. Choice A is not a macroeconomic variable, because it is examining an individual market. Choices B, C, D, and E examine larger issues like national income levels, a country's unemployment rate, all exports for a country, and the national average price level.

Chapter 6: Measurement of Economic Systems

31. (E) Choice E is the best answer because it states that workers, entrepreneurs, and owners of capital all offer their services through a resource market (a market used to exchange the services of resources of land, labor, and capital). A product market in Choice A refers to the mechanism used to exchange goods and services. The circular flow model also incorporates the role of the government and the foreign sector.

32. (A) In the circular flow model, households serve as the buyers of finished products and the sellers of resources. Businesses are the buyers of resources and the sellers of finished products. Choice A would be the best answer. Choices B, D, and E are incorrect because businesses are sellers of products and demanders of resources. Choice C is incorrect because GDP is calculated through either the income or expenditure approach.

33. (A) The circular flow model shows how households, individuals, and businesses circulate resources, goods, and income throughout the economy.

34. (A) The GDP refers to all final goods produced in an economy for a one-year period. Intermediate goods are not counted in the GDP, to avoid double counting. Choice D is incorrect because the GDP does not calculate domestic businesses in foreign locations; so a McDonald's located in London, England, would be left out. Choice E is incorrect because it is only half of the equation to calculate GDP.

35. (C) Choice C is the best answer because GDP does not calculate domestic businesses abroad, whereas that is calculated in the GNP.

36. (A) Choice C is incorrect because it refers only to consumers, whereas the question is asking about businesses. Choice B is incorrect because supply refers to the amount firms are willing to produce at each possible price level. Choices D and E are incorrect because they do not relate to the amounts firms are willing to invest.

37. (A) A leakage in the circular flow model is anything that would decrease the consumption of goods and services. Taxes would decrease consumer's purchasing power and a firm's production output. The same goes for an individual's or household's savings.

38. (C) Intermediate goods are not counted in the GDP, to avoid double counting. A computer chip, lumber, and a used car would succumb to double counting if they were calculated into the GDP. So the best answer would be Choice C, a new car.

39. (A) Housing, education, and health insurance are goods and services that both consumers and producers provide. For example, housing may be subsidized the state or federal government; students may attend either a public school paid for by taxes, or a private school paid for by private tuition; and health insurances such as Medicare and Medicaid are government programs, but an individual may choose to pay out of pocket.

40. (B) The construction of a car engine would not be calculated into the GDP, because the final sale of the car it goes into would incorporate all intermediate expenses incurred in the building of the vehicle. Choice B would be the best answer. All other choices are final products that would be calculated into the GDP.

41. (D) You must know the formula for calculating GDP: $C + I + G + (X - M)$. C represents consumer spending; I represents investments by businesses; G represents government spending; and X represents exports and M represents imports. Savings are not calculated into the GDP.

42. (A) The circular flow model is often expanded to illustrate the role government plays in the distribution of goods and services throughout the economy. If the government is added into the circular flow model, it indicates it is participating in providing goods and services to businesses and households.

43. (E) You must know the formula for calculating GDP: C + I + G + (X − M). Choice E is the best answer, whereas Choices A, B, C, and D would represent miscalculations. Refer to question 41.

44. (C) Although Jason and Mary take out a loan and spend a significant portion of their savings on the purchase of a new home, this would be calculated as an investment. Purchase of real estate, such as a house or a condominium, would be calculated in the GDP as investment because all homeowners want their properties to increase in value and see a positive return if they choose to sell the house in the future.

45. (B) Investments are a part of calculating GDP. National accountants would say that the GDP increased by $100 billion (Choice B). All other choices are either miscalculations or do not factor investments into the GDP.

46. (A) If you know the formula for calculating GDP, then this question should be no problem. Personal consumption, the difference between exports and imports, and domestic and government investments are all calculated in the GDP. All other factors in the chart are not considered in the GDP.

47. (B) Nominal GDP is defined as the value of production at current prices, whereas real GDP is the value of production using prices at a fixed point in time. Choice B is the best answer because it explains a change in value over time.

48. (D) A simple equation would be used to answer this question: nominal GDP/price index or 200/0.90 = 222 billion. All other choices are incorrect due to miscalculations.

49. (E) The labor force is defined as all individuals 16 years and older who are currently employed or unemployed. People who are not actively looking for work are not considered part of the labor force.

50. (A) The labor force is defined as all individuals 16 years and older who are currently employed or unemployed. People who are not actively looking for work are not considered part of the labor force.

51. (B) Frictional unemployment is created through turnover in the labor market, or when existing workers leave their jobs to look for better ones. Elaine quitting her job to go back to school and look for a better job places her as frictionally unemployed.

52. (A) Cyclical unemployment occurs when there are too few jobs due to an economic downturn. If structural and frictional unemployment are at a minimum and cyclical unemployment is zero, it is said the economy is approaching full employment.

53. (B) The consumer price index measures changes in the price level of consumer goods and services. The producer price index measures average changes in the price level of produced goods by producers. Calculating changes in the price levels for consumer goods and the output by producers, economists have a better understanding of the rate of inflation.

54. (C) Stagflation occurs in the macro-economy when inflation and the unemployment rate are both increasing. Real GDP is also decreasing at this time. This is also known as cost-push inflation.

55. (A) Cyclical unemployment occurs when there are too few jobs due to an economic downturn. If a teacher loses his or her job due to a decrease in the student population living in the district, the economy is doing poorly.

56. (C) The unemployment rate is calculated as the number of unemployed workers/ total labor force × 100. In this case, 1,000/9,000 × 100 = 11%. All other choices are miscalculations.

57. (B) Remember, the labor force does not calculate the number of people not working. The labor force is defined as all individuals 16 years and older who are currently employed or unemployed. People who are not actively looking for work are not considered part of the labor force.

58. (E) The sale of a bicycle would be included in the GDP for that year. The 10 remaining bicycles would not be considered part of the GDP. Therefore, 90 bicycles × $50 = $4,500 added to the GDP.

59. (D) Supply-side economists support stimulating aggregate supply by promoting policies that encourage investment and entrepreneurship. Such policies would enact tax breaks that would increase disposable incomes, and hopefully increase household savings and investments in businesses. Choice A is incorrect because that money could be used as tax breaks for individuals. Choice B is incorrect because that would stimulate aggregate demand, not supply. Choice C is incorrect because a decrease in government spending and investment often leads to increased unemployment.

60. (B) If Dennis wants a 5% return on his loan, he should add the real interest rate plus the rate of inflation, or 15 + 5 = 20%.

61. (E) The gross domestic product is the market value for all goods and services produced within a country for a year. The GDP does not consider businesses on foreign soil. Therefore, a McDonalds operating in England would not be part of the U.S. GDP. It would be considered part of England's GDP. Gross national product is the GDP plus all output produced abroad.

62. (E) The labor force is employed workers plus unemployed workers. Since Jessica has recently graduated from college but has not yet taken the job at IBM, this would leave the labor force unchanged.

63. (E) People who are not actively looking for work are not considered part of the labor force.

64. (A) Choice A is the best answer because hyperinflation describes an extremely rapid increase in prices. A gradual increase of prices over time would not be considered hyperinflation. Choice C is not the correct answer because the value of money falls during hyperinflation.

65. (E) Remember the formula for calculating GDP: C + I + G + (X – M). You must plug in the numbers and find what is missing to answer this question, where C = $4 million, I = $2 million, G = $5 million, and X is $4 million: 4 + 2 + 5 + (4 – ?) = $15 million.

66. (A) Choice A is the best answer because marshmallows used in ice cream would be considered an intermediate good. Choices B, C, D, and E are all considered final goods.

67. (B) Choice B is the best answer because establishing a price index helps economists, businesses, and the government compare prices over time. Establishing a rate of inflation and nominal prices versus real prices would not be necessary without a base year of comparison. Choice A is incorrect because it refers to the GDP price deflator. Choice C is incorrect because it refers to inflation. Choice D is incorrect because it refers to the peak of a business cycle.

68. (D) The underground economy refers to both illegal activities and economic activities unreported. Choice D is the best answer because the sale of a used car at a car dealership is neither illegal nor unreported.

69. (C) Nominal GDP refers to the current value of output using current prices. It is different from real GDP because real GDP measures the value of current output compared to prices at a fixed point in time.

Chapter 7: National Income and Price Determination

70. (B) The aggregate demand curve follows the law of demand: consumers are less willing and able to purchase a good or service as price increases, and vice versa. The aggregate demand curve shows at which price levels consumers are willing and able to buy goods and services.

71. (E) The real-balances effect states that as price levels increase, the purchasing power of money decreases, which decreases consumption. This reflects an inverse relationship. The interest rate effect states that as interest rates rise, there is a reduction in total capital investment and would result in a decrease in aggregate demand. Choices A and B would contribute to the downward slope of the aggregate demand curve. The substitution effect shows how as price increases for a good, substitute products will increase in demand. The crowding out effect states that interest rates will rise due to increased government borrowing.

72. (A) Any rightward shift of a supply or demand curve will result in economic growth. In this question, economic growth occurred from AS1 to AS2.

73. (A) Full employment refers to the ability for all individuals willing and able to work to be employed. The idea of full employment coincides with long-run aggregate supply, where the long-run production point equals the full-employment level.

74. (A) Intermediate goods are not counted in the GDP to avoid double counting. The GDP calculates the sale of all final goods and services.

75. (C) The multiplier effect explains any change in spending, such as consumer consumption, investment, or government spending, that has a greater effect on actual output.

76. (B) Choice B is the best answer because a change in price level will reflect only a change in the quantity demanded and not an actual shift of the aggregate demand curve. Choices A, C, D, and E are all determinants of aggregate demand that could shift the curve to the left or right.

77. (A) A rightward shift of the aggregate supply curve represents economic growth. So Choice C is incorrect because increased government regulations would restrict output and cause a leftward shift of the curve. Choice D is incorrect because that would shift only the aggregate demand curve to the right. Choice B is incorrect because that would increase costs for producers and therefore shift the curve to the left. Choice A is the best answer because an increase in productivity increases output and would shift the curve to the right.

78. (B) This is the definition of an aggregate supply curve. According to the law of supply, producers are willing and able to produce more at higher price levels, and vice versa. This reflects a direct relationship between price and output.

79. (B) A leftward shift of the aggregate supply curve shows a decrease in economic output. If workers' wages decreased, a major cost to producers would decrease. This would push the aggregate supply curve to the right.

80. (C) The interest rate effect states that as interest rates rise, there is a reduction in total capital investment, and this would result in a decrease in aggregate demand. As the price level increases, so do interest rates because consumers are attempting to borrow more money.

81. (A) The multiplier effect explains any change in spending, such as consumer consumption, investment, or government spending, which has a greater effect on actual output. The multiplier effect is not strongly felt if the price level rises and weakens the impact of increased spending.

82. (E) You must use the formula $1/(1 - MPC)$, or $1/0.2 = 5$. Then $5 \times \$10$ billion = an increase of $50 billion.

83. (C) Choice C is the best answer because if supply decreases while demand for a good or service increases, an increase in the price level will result.

84. (A) Many businesses choose to reduce employment due to government regulations regarding a minimum wage. Wages are a huge cost to producers, and they choose to lay off workers rather than reduce wages. Choice B is incorrect because reducing employment does not increase the cost of production. Choice C is incorrect because reducing employment does not create inflation, although it may be the result of inflation. Choices D and E are unrelated to a reduction in employment over a reduction in wages.

85. (B) The long-run aggregate supply curve is vertical in the long run. The long run represents enough time for producers to make adjustments to production and workers' wages to adjust to real wages.

86. (C) Stagflation exists when inflation and unemployment increase at the same time. Choice C is the best answer because supply shock is a drastic and rapid change to the determinants of aggregate supply. If an event occurs, such as cost-push inflation or a new government regulation, this may affect aggregate supply, thus affecting the inflation rate and unemployment rate.

87. (C) Choice A is incorrect because it refers to the recessionary gap. Choice B is incorrect because it refers to the inflationary gap. Choice D is incorrect because it refers to deflation. Choice E is incorrect because it refers to a recession. Choice C is correct because equilibrium will always refer to the point where total output demanded equals total output supplied.

88. (A) Choice A is the best answer because an increase in government spending will show an increase in the calculation of GDP: G = government spending in C + I + G + (X – M). All other choices reflect a decrease in specific parts of the economy.

89. (B) Choice B is the correct answer because a recessionary gap refers to the amount by which full-employment GDP exceeds the equilibrium of real GDP. Choice A is incorrect because an inflationary gap refers to the amount by which equilibrium at real GDP exceeds full employment. Choice C is incorrect because it refers to a rapid and drastic increase in the price level. Choice D is incorrect because it refers to where inflation and unemployment increase at the same time. Choice E is incorrect because it refers to the GDP falling for six consecutive months.

90. (A) The Phillips curve illustrates the inverse relationship between unemployment and inflation. The lower the unemployment, the higher the rate of inflation, and vice versa. Just as the aggregate supply curve in the long run, the Phillips curve is vertical in the long run.

91. (C) The Phillips curve illustrates the inverse relationship between unemployment and inflation. The lower the unemployment, the higher the rate of inflation, and vice versa.

92. (A) The market forces of aggregate supply and aggregate demand indicate the point of full employment, where all individuals who are willing and able to work are employed.

93. (D) The multiplier effect explains any change in spending—such as consumer consumption, investment, or government spending—that has a greater effect on actual output.

94. (B) You must use the formula $1/(1 - MPC)$, or $1/(1 - 0.7) = 3.3$. Then $3.3 \times 5 = \$16.5$ billion increase in real GDP.

95. (A) The crowding out effect involves government borrowing to fund government spending. The choices that do not refer to the government may be disregarded. When the government increases its borrowing, it essentially crowds out private investment. Therefore, the real connection is between government borrowing/spending and private investment and consumption.

96. (C) The answer to this question involves a rightward shift of the aggregate demand curve, so you are looking for actions that would increase the GDP. Choice C is the best answer because an increase in government spending will result in an increase in the GDP. All other choices involve contracting the GDP.

97. (A) A supply shock is an event or action that rapidly increases or decrease total output, shifting the aggregate supply curve to the left or right. Choice A is the best answer because discovery of new resources would increase the amount of total output very quickly. Choices B, C, and D would occur over a longer period of time.

98. (A) The multiplier effect explains any change in spending—such as consumer consumption, investment, or government spending—that has a greater effect on actual output. The question asks for the effect of an increase in government spending, which would increase the GDP; so any answer that results in a decrease should be eliminated.

99. (B) A supply shock is an event or action that rapidly increases or decrease total output, shifting the aggregate supply curve to the left or right. A negative supply shock would push the aggregate supply curve to the left. Choice B is the only diagram that represents this scenario.

100. (A) The long-run aggregate supply (LRAS) curve is vertical because enough time has passed for total output to adjust to the price level. At this point, it is assumed that the LRAS is independent of changes in price, and output is determined by other factors of production.

101. (A) Gross domestic product (GDP) is an excellent measure of the health of a nation's economy by measuring the total amount of income generated in a country for a year. Choices B, C, and D are irrelevant when questioning what the GDP indicates.

102. (C) This is another multiplier question. You must use the formula $1/(1 - MPC)$ or $1/(1 - 0.6) = 2.5$. Then $2.5 \times 10 = \$25$ billion.

103. (B) The consumer price index measures the average price level using a base year. It is the best measure of consumer inflation. Choice B would be the best answer if one were to check the rate of inflation in the economy.

104. (B) One of the main tactics used to battle the Great Depression was an increase in government spending. Increasing government spending would increase the GDP and result in a shift of the aggregate demand curve to the right. Therefore, any answer with a decrease in government spending should be eliminated. If there is an increase in taxes, there would be less consumer consumption because people would have less disposable income. Choice B is the best answer.

105. (E) This is another multiplier question. You must use the formula $1/(1 - MPC)$ or $1/(1 - 0.6) = 2.5$. Then $25/2.5 = \$10$ billion in government spending.

Chapter 8: Financial Sector

106. (A) Choice A is the best answer because out of the three functions of money, Jay is using it as a unit of account. This means that money is being used as a standard of measurement for the value or cost of goods and services. Choice B is incorrect because a medium of exchange is an intermediary used in the exchange of goods and services, such as paper money used to purchase a drum set. Choice C is incorrect because a store of value is any form of commodity, asset, or money that has value and can be stored away and retrieved at a later time. Choice E is incorrect because M2 money refers to a category of money: M1 money plus savings, time-related deposits, and noninstitutional money market funds.

107. (B) One of the best benefits of using money as a medium of exchange is its standardization of use. Bartering becomes difficult when two people cannot agree on the value of the goods they are exchanging. Using money as a medium of exchange simplifies economic operations greatly.

108. (B) M1 money refers to all coins and paper currency and all money in checking accounts (checkable deposits). This is the most readily available form of money. Choices A, C, and D are part of M2 money.

109. (D) A bond represents a debt from the issuer to the person to whom the bond is made. People buy U.S. bonds, and the government promises to pay back that money plus interest after a certain period of time.

110. (E) Choice E is the best answer because M1 money refers to all coins and paper currency and all money in checking accounts (checkable deposits).

111. (D) M3 money includes M1 and M2 money and all institutional money market accounts and large time deposits. The M3 money supply is used to calculate the entire money supply in an economy. Therefore, Choice D is the best answer because all of the items are part of M3.

112. (B) Choice B is the best answer because checkable deposits are part of the M1 money supply: money that is the most liquid and easily accessible. Therefore, M1 would increase and M2 and M3 would remain the same.

113. (C) The money used in the United States is backed and supported by the U.S. government. The United States does not have a gold standard anymore (Choice D), nor is it backed by valuable land (Choice B). Money has value because the U.S. government decrees it does.

114. (A) The consumer price index (CPI) measures changes in the price level of consumer goods and services. Therefore, the purchasing power of the dollar is also measured through the CPI. The steps needed to answer this question are as follows: 90 (base year) divided by 120 (target year) and multiplied by 100, or $90/120 \times 100 = 75$. Subtract 75 from 100 to calculate the percent change in the purchasing power of the dollar between these two time periods. In this case, the purchasing power of the dollar fell by 25%.

115. (A) If the interest rate decreased, as set by the Federal Reserve Bank, the amount of available assets would increase. Consumers would have more money available to them.

116. (B) There is an inverse relationship between the price of bonds and the established interest rate. This is so because if you bought a bond for $100 with a 5% interest rate and the interest rate drops to 4% over the next few years, then you lost a 1% value on that bond.

117. (A) The Federal Open Market Committee (FOMC) is part of the Federal Reserve System where a board of governors meets to decide monetary policy. They decide to either increase or decrease the money supply by buying/selling government securities or raising/lowering interest rates.

118. (B) Interest rates are used when consumers purchase goods and services with credit. The consumer may purchase the good or service and not pay all at once, but then the consumer must pay more money based on the established interest rate. If the interest rate falls, more and more people would make purchases, like a house, using credit.

119. (A) The Federal Reserve System utilizes monetary policy to control the money supply and stimulate the economy. In order to decrease or increase the money supply, a main tool of the Fed is to buy and sell government securities from commercial banks. Choices B, C, D, and E are all functions of the Fed, but Choice A is the most significant.

120. (E) M1 money refers to all coins and paper currency and all money in checking accounts (checkable deposits). The most significant characteristic of M1 money is that it is held by the public. Institutions like the federal government and the Fed would not be a part of M1 money supply.

121. (A) Money is created when the Federal Reserve prints money to buy government securities. This money is sent out to the U.S. Treasury and then dispersed through economic operations. When a loan is repaid, the money ceases to exist because the debt that created the money is paid back.

122. (B) If interest rates increase, more money is required to pay back loans, from mortgage payments on a house to everyday purchases with a credit card. This would constrict the money supply, and the demand for money would decrease.

123. (A) Members of the Federal Reserve Board are elected to 14-year terms. This long span of time gives each member freedom from political pressure. This time gives board members the freedom to make rational judgments regarding monetary policy.

124. (C) A bank's total reserves are the actual amount the bank has on hand in its vaults and any money on reserve at the Fed. Choice C is the best answer because it calculates the bank's cash and money on reserve at the Fed. All other choices are miscalculations.

125. (A) Remember that money is created through debt. If a loan is made to an individual for $5,000, then the bank created that amount of money into the money supply. Leo's initial deposit would only increase the M1 money supply.

126. (C) Liquidity refers to the degree to which an asset is bought or sold in the market with the greatest ease possible. Liquidity is highly related to trading and is the preferred state for trading because it is easier for investors to pull or put money into trade. Liquidity is often at odds with profits due to market fluctuations.

127. (C) A major problem of banks that led to the Great Depression was the lack of monitoring and influence by the government. Requiring banks to have a percentage of their money on reserve is a method of controlling and influencing the banks. Choice C is the best answer.

128. (A) One of the main and most significant goals of monetary policy instituted by the Federal Reserve Bank is to help the economy grow or contract based on the current state of the economy. The economy goes through a business cycle: expansion, peak, contraction, trough, and recovery. Varying the money supply (to help the economy grow or contract) is a valuable tool of the Federal Reserve.

129. (C) M1 money refers to all coins and paper currency and all money in checking accounts (checkable deposits). This is the most readily available form of money.

130. (A) M2 money is M1 money plus savings, time-related deposits, and noninstitutional money market funds.

131. (A) The money from S1 to S2 represents a decrease in the money supply. Any answer that references an increase should be eliminated. When the money supply decreases, the Fed is instituting a tight money policy, which would contract the economy. One significant way to implement this is for the Fed to purchase government securities.

132. (C) Choice C is the best answer because usually the Fed institutes a contractionary monetary policy as a way to battle inflation. If prices are too high, then the money supply is too high; therefore, the Fed should reduce the money supply to combat inflation.

133. (D) Transactions demand and assets demand comprise the two components for the demand for money. Transaction demand is money kept for purchases and has a direct relationship with the GDP; asset demand is money kept for a store of value for later use and is inversely related with the GDP.

134. (A) A stock is a certified piece of paper that represents a claim of ownership in a business.

135. (A) A bond represents a debt from the issuer to the person to whom the bond is made. People buy U.S. bonds, and the government promises to pay back that money plus interest after a certain period of time.

136. (E) The quantity theory of money states that as the money supply increases, higher prices will result and not affect real output. Choice A is incorrect because it describes the money multiplier. Choice B is incorrect because it refers to the federal funds rate. Choice C is incorrect because it refers to half of the equation to calculate the exchange rate. Choice D is incorrect because it refers to the velocity of money.

137. (A) Choice A is the best answer because it represents the quantity theory of money: as the money supply increases, higher prices will result and not affect real output.

138. (A) Choice A is the best answer because debt financing is the method by which firms raise investment by issuing bonds to the public. Remember that money is created through debt.

139. (A) Choice A is the best answer because it correctly calculates the money multiplier, or 1/RR or 1/0.1 = 10. Then 10 × 500 = $5,000 in money creation. All other answers are miscalculations.

140. (B) Choice B is the best answer because a unit of account is money being used as a standard of measurement for the value and/or cost of goods and services.

141. (E) Choice E is the best answer because a medium of exchange is an intermediary used in the exchange of goods and services, such as paper money.

142. (C) The Federal Reserve System is responsible for implementing monetary policy. Choices A, B, D, and E are all facets of monetary policy, whereas Choice C refers to tax rates, which is part of fiscal policy and is implemented by the federal government.

143. (C) Choice C is the best answer because cash withdrawals are now in the possession of whoever took the money and is free to use it as he or she pleases. An asset of the bank is anything owned by the bank. Choices A, B, D, and E are assets that belong to a bank.

144. (B) Something that has value in itself and is also used as a form of money is known as commodity money. A gold coin is commodity money: it is valuable both as gold and as a form of medium of exchange.

145. (C) The central bank of the United States is the Federal Reserve Bank. It is responsible for regulating monetary policy and the financial system.

146. (A) M1 money refers to all coins and paper currency and all money in checking accounts (checkable deposits). Travelers' checks are often used as cash by people on vacation and would therefore be part of the M1 money supply.

147. (A) Choice A is the best answer because it correctly calculates the money multiplier, $1/0.05 = 20$.

148. (C) Choice C is the best answer because increasing the reserve ratio will decrease the money supply. If banks are required to increase the amount of cash they must keep in their vaults, then that decreases the lending power of the bank. If banks are making fewer loans out to businesses and individuals, then the money supply will decrease.

149. (A) Remember that there is an inverse relationship between the price of a bond and inflation.

150. (E) Choice E is the best answer because a bank's biggest liability is checkable deposits. The banks are responsible for being able to provide and account for that money on hand. Remember that checkable deposits are part of M1 money, which is the most liquid and available form of money in an economy.

Chapter 9: Inflation, Unemployment, and Stabilization Policies

151. (E) Choice E is the best answer because Choices A, B, C, and D refer to monetary policy regulated by the Federal Reserve System. Fiscal policy is implemented by the federal government through taxes and spending/investment.

152. (A) A contractionary fiscal policy aims to decrease inflation by decreasing aggregate demand and supply. Increasing taxes will decrease consumption, while decreasing government spending, as part of the formula for the GDP, will shift the aggregate supply curve to the left.

153. (B) Choice B is the best answer because this is a contractionary fiscal policy. When the government implements a contractionary fiscal policy, it is usually trying to deal with high prices brought on by inflation.

154. (C) Choice C is the best answer because discretionary fiscal policy refers to actions taken by the federal government that do not happen automatically. Choice A is irrelevant to this question. Choice B would be the exact opposite of what the government hopes to achieve. Choice D is incorrect because nondiscretionary fiscal policy refers to changes in government expenditures that happen automatically without government implementation. Choice E is incorrect because monetary policy is regulated by the Fed.

155. (A) A decrease in aggregate demand is represented by a leftward shift of the aggregate demand curve. This would result from a tight, or contractionary, fiscal policy.

156. (C) Remember that when the government implements a tax, it serves as a transfer of money from the people to the government; when the government increases government spending, it serves as a transfer of money from the government to the people. Having both a decrease in taxes and government spending would, therefore, counteract each other.

157. (A) Demand-pull inflation refers to inflation caused by an increasing aggregate demand (AD) as it moves toward the upward sloping range of aggregate supply. Therefore, the goal is to move the AD curve from AD3 to AD2, which necessitates a contractionary fiscal policy. Choice A is the best answer because increasing taxes would decrease purchasing power of consumers and thus decrease aggregate demand.

158. (D) Because you are looking for an increase in real GDP, you may disregard any answer that suggests a decrease in government spending. This would result in a rightward shift of the AD curve, and the only viable option is Choice D.

159. (B) If the country is in a recession, then the government wants to stimulate the economy by increasing the GDP. This requires an increase to one of the determinants of calculating the GDP: consumer spending, investment, government spending, and the difference between exports and imports. Therefore, you may disregard any answer that elects to decrease government spending. Choices A and D are incorrect because these two policies would counteract each other. Choice B is the best answer.

160. (A) This is another multiplier question, and the formula is $1/(1 - MPC)$, but remember that the question gave the marginal propensity to save ($MPS = 0.4$), so this must be subtracted from 1 to get the marginal propensity to consume ($MPC = 0.6$). $1/(1 - 0.6) = 1/(0.4) = 2.5$. $2.5x = 50$ billion. If the government wished to increase the aggregate demand by \$50 billion, then it should increase government spending by \$20 billion.

161. (D) The crowding out effect may be avoided if the government issues new money; an increase in government spending "crowds out" private businesses and consumers from investment. If new money is introduced into the economy, then this may be avoided, but it comes at the price of depreciation.

162. (A) If the government is experiencing a deficit, then the total amount of government expenditures is greater than revenue generated. If the government is increasing the amount of its expenditures, then the crowding out effect may occur. One way to avoid the crowding out effect is for the government to issue new money. This new money then becomes available to private investors, although the downside is depreciation due to more money in the money supply.

163. (D) A built-in stabilizer will act automatically without specific policy actions of the government. Transfer payments refer to payments made by the government for social welfare programs. If income increases, then transfer payments tend to decrease.

164. (E) Choice E is the best answer because if the economy is at full employment, disposable income will increase and result in inflation due to the increase in consumers' purchasing power.

165. (A) The crowding out effect involves government borrowing to fund government spending.

166. (B) Choices C and D refer to monetary policy, which is regulated by the Fed, so these answer may be eliminated because the question refers to fiscal policy. Choice B is the best answer because an expansionary policy will increase aggregate demand. As a result, the dollar will appreciate and make goods and services more expensive to foreigners. Therefore, net exports will tend to fall with an expansionary policy.

167. **(A)** A progressive tax system refers to how the proportion of taxes paid increases with an increase in income. This is the only acceptable answer out of the choices.

168. **(A)** A contractionary fiscal policy is aiming to decrease aggregate demand. The answer that would most reduce one of the components for calculating the GDP is Choice A.

169. **(D)** Demand-pull inflation refers to inflation caused by an increasing aggregate demand as it moves toward the upward sloping range of aggregate supply. If there is an increase in the money supply, an increase in aggregate demand will result.

170. **(C)** Cost-push inflation refers to an increase in price level due to an increase in the costs of production. Cost-push inflation will occur if no gains in productivity are seen.

171. **(A)** Just like the LRAS curve, the Phillips curve will be vertical in the long run. The Phillips curve measures the inverse relationship between inflation and unemployment. With economic growth, inflation increases, which should lead to an increase in employment.

172. **(A)** The long-run aggregate supply curve is vertical in the long run. The long run represents enough time for producers to make adjustments to production and workers' wages to adjust to real wages. All other choices will have an effect on real GDP.

173. **(D)** If GDP falls for two consecutive quarters, then the society is in an official recession.

174. **(B)** The Federal Reserve Bank is responsible for maintaining the money supply for the United States. The federal government controls fiscal policy, which involves taxes and government spending and borrowing.

175. **(A)** The idea behind monetization is the actions of the Federal Reserve Bank to print more money and increase the money supply. Any increase in the money supply will result in inflation, so any choice that refers to decreasing inflation may be eliminated. Choice C is incorrect because selling government securities would contract the economy.

176. **(A)** Choice A is the best answer because selling government securities would decrease the money supply and as a result decrease inflation. Choices D and E are incorrect because income taxes are included only in fiscal policy.

177. **(C)** An expansionary monetary policy aims to increase the money supply and increase aggregate demand. As a result, employment will increase. Choice C is the best answer.

178. **(A)** You must use the money multiplier to answer this questions. $1/(1 - MPC)$ or $1/(1 - 0.7) = 1/0.3 = 3.33$. Then $3.33 \times 10 = 33$ billion.

179. (A) Choice A is the best answer because monetary policy works quickly to increase or decrease aggregate demand as compared to the length of time it takes for the effects of taxes and government spending to be felt in the economy.

180. (B) A contractionary monetary policy is being implemented when securities are being sold. As a result, the lending power of a commercial bank decreases due to less money in the money supply.

181. (A) The discount rate refers to the interest rate the Fed sets for loans given out to commercial banks. As the rate is decreased, more commercial banks will seek loans from the Fed. If the Fed is selling government securities, then a contractionary monetary policy is being implemented, which results in a tighter money supply. It would therefore be counterproductive to lower the discount rate at the same time.

182. (E) If the economy is experiencing high unemployment and low economic growth, then it would be best to stimulate the economy to encourage growth. Therefore, the Fed should pursue an easy money policy and buy government securities.

183. (B) If the Fed is implementing a tight money policy, then it is trying to combat inflation. One way to combat inflation is to decrease the money supply by pursuing a tight money policy.

184. (C) The discount rate refers to the interest rate the Fed sets to loans given out to commercial banks. As the rate is decreased, more commercial banks will seek loans from the Fed. This would help stimulate the economy.

185. (A) Choice A is the best answer because if the country is experiencing high unemployment, then one way monetary and fiscal policy could help is to increase aggregate demand by pursuing expansionary policies. So look for the answer that suggests buying government securities and increasing government spending.

186. (C) If the Fed is buying government securities, then it is pursuing an expansionary money policy, thus trying to stimulate the economy and economic growth. Buying securities increases the money supply—in this case by $50 million.

187. (E) The velocity of money refers to the average number of times per year a dollar is spent. A reason why this would be a disadvantage is the fact that the velocity of money may be unpredictable. For example, a tight money policy might cause people to spend money faster, causing velocity to rise and providing a skewed picture.

188. (A) On the Federal Reserve's consolidated balance sheet, securities are listed as the biggest asset.

189. (B) An easy money policy seeks to increase aggregate demand. The major method the Fed has to implement this policy is buying government securities, which would increase the money supply and push the aggregate demand curve to the right.

190. (A) Demand-pull inflation refers to inflation caused by an increasing aggregate demand as it moves toward the upward sloping range of aggregate supply.

191. (C) Cost-push inflation deals with aggregate supply, so you may eliminate this choice due to the nature of the diagram provided. Choice B is incorrect because it refers to naturally occurring inflation over a gradual course of time. Choices D and E are incorrect because only aggregate demand and supply are represented in the diagram. Choice C is the best answer because demand-pull inflation refers to inflation caused by an increasing aggregate demand as it moves toward the upward sloping range of aggregate supply.

192. (A) Demand-pull inflation refers to aggregate demand, so you may eliminate this choice based on the nature of the diagram. Cost-push inflation deals with aggregate supply and an increase in price level due to an increase in the costs of production. Therefore, the diagram shows an increase in aggregate supply and an inflation of price.

193. (A) Cost-push inflation deals with aggregate supply and an increase in price level due to an increase in the costs of production.

194. (A) If the economy is in a recession, then the government will attempt to stimulate aggregate demand through expansionary fiscal and monetary policies. If the economy is experiencing inflation, then the government will attempt to contract the money supply and bring the overall price level down.

195. (B) Built-in, or automatic, stabilizers are part of nondiscretionary fiscal policy, where no action is needed from the policy makers to make a change to government spending or borrowing.

196. (D) Built-in, or automatic, stabilizers are part of nondiscretionary fiscal policy, where no action is needed from the policy makers to make a change to government spending or borrowing.

197. (A) Choice A is the best answer because recognition lag is the delay in which an event or shock is felt or noticed by society. This may result in a lag in implementing counteracting monetary and fiscal policies.

198. (A) Built-in, or automatic, stabilizers are part of nondiscretionary fiscal policy, where no action is needed from the policy makers to make a change to government spending or borrowing.

199. (D) If the costs of production lead to an increase in the cost of a good or service without an increase in overall production, it is said to be cost-push inflation.

200. (C) The Federal Reserve System has three main tools: buying/selling government securities, the discount rate, and the reserve ratio. These three tools are very powerful in implementing fast-acting monetary policy.

201. **(A)** Increasing the discount rate will discourage commercial banks from borrowing money from the Fed due to the high interest rate, and money creation will be slowed. Choice A is the best answer.

202. **(A)** The crowding out effect states that interest rates will rise due to increased government borrowing. The scenario in this question is a result of government borrowing. If the government chooses to increase borrowing to fund additional spending, this will result in crowding out private investors.

203. **(C)** Lowering the discount rate would encourage commercial banks to borrow more from the Fed, and money creation will increase.

204. **(D)** If the Fed lowered the reserve ratio, then the amount of money commercial banks are required to keep on reserve would decrease. This means there is more money to be lent out in the form of investments and loans.

205. **(C)** This is a basic definition of the velocity of money.

Chapter 10: Economic Growth and Productivity

206. **(A)** Per capita GDP represents the total output a country produces in a year divided by the total population. GDP can be calculated by adding up the population's income for the year. Choice A is the best answer because if per capita GDP increases, then it signals an increase in the standard of living for that country. Choice B is incorrect because a decrease in the standard of living would not coincide with an increase in per capita GDP. Choice C is incorrect because contractionary measures taken by the Fed are meant to decrease inflation. Choices D and E are incorrect because this would occur when the economy is in a downturn.

207. **(B)** You must use the Rule of 70 to answer this question. The Rule of 70 is used when economists want to know how long it will take real GDP to double, thus knowing the effectiveness of economic growth measures. The Rule of 70 is 70/annual percent rate of growth. Therefore, 70/2 = 35 years. Choices A, C, D, and E are all miscalculations.

208. **(E)** Choice E is the best answer because an increasing inflation rate would contract the economy, and the Federal Reserve and federal government would implement tight monetary and fiscal policies. Choices A, B, C, and D all influence a growing economy.

209. **(A)** Utilizing resources in the best way to maximize a society's benefit is a better answer compared to Choice B. Utilizing resources in the cheapest way possible is good, but if it comes at a greater cost than benefit to a society, then it is poor economic practice. Choice C refers to the Rule of 70. Choice D follows the same function as Choice B. Choice E is incorrect because any point outside the production possibilities curve is unattainable with the current state of resources.

210. **(C)** The Rule of 70 is used when economists want to know how long it will take real GDP to double, thus knowing the effectiveness of economic growth measures.

211. (E) You must know the definition of per capita GDP to answer this question. Per capita GDP represents the total output a country produces in a year divided by the total population.

212. (A) Choices B, D, and E are incorrect because they refer to the factors of production. The question states economic growth without a change in the factors of production, so these choices should be eliminated immediately. Choice A is the best answer because for an economy to increase its output without increasing any of the factors of production, new technologies must be utilized to increase output.

213. (E) A good measure economists use to compare a country's standard of living and wealth is calculating per capita GDP, which is the total GDP divided by the total population. A high per capita GDP reflects a high standard of living, because one way to calculate GDP is to total the incomes in the country for the year.

214. (C) Human capital refers to the knowledge and skills a worker possesses. The worker contributes this knowledge and skills to the work that he or she does. Receiving education training for a job is an increase in human capital. Choice A is incorrect because it refers to the flow of investment on financial assets.

215. (A) Choice A is the best answer because it reflects the relationship between capital (a factor of production) and GDP: if one of the factors of production increases, GDP will increase along with wages. All other answers should be dismissed because they reflect a decrease or no change in GDP with an increase in capital stock.

216. (A) Choice A is the best answer because per capita GDP is calculated by dividing GDP by the total population. If the population increases, the denominator increases, thus giving a smaller number. Also, an increase in the population will lead to an increase in the labor force over the period of five years. This will then increase real GDP.

217. (D) Choice D is the best answer because this idea reflects supply-side economics, where policies give tax breaks to the wealthy so they can take that money and invest, therefore creating an increase in production and economic growth.

Chapter 11: International Trade and Finance

218. (B) Choice B is the best answer because the goal of an import quota is to limit the amount of foreign goods entering a country. If the supply is limited, prices will be higher for those imports than domestic goods. Prices will be higher for consumers, and domestic producers of motorbikes have a better chance of selling their products.

219. (E) A capital account shows the flow of investment of real or financial assets between two nations. A balance of payment is a summary of payments received and sent between a nation and a foreign nation. The key to answering this question is to find the answer that has a relationship between two nations. Choice E is the only choice that reflects this dynamic.

220. (E) Choice E is the best answer because if the Chinese economy is growing, then there is an increase in demand for U.S. goods, which increases the value of the U.S. dollar. The yuan would depreciate.

221. (B) Choice B is the best answer because as interest rates increase, it becomes more expensive to borrow money for capital, such as machinery and equipment. Therefore, capital investments will decrease. However, as interest rates increase, financial investments, such as bonds, increase as well; the income received on financial investments increases.

222. (D) A tariff is a tax placed on foreign goods as a way to protect domestic producers.

223. (D) Choice D is the best answer because even though the nation of XYZ produces bananas, if the world price is lower than the domestic price, a shortage is created. The nation of XYZ will import cheaper foreign bananas to correct the domestic shortage.

224. (B) Choice B is the best answer because it correctly defines a current account. A current account shows payments on imports and exports of goods and services and investment income sent abroad and received by the United States. Therefore, if there was a surplus in the current account, that means more investments from abroad came into the United States than export investments went out.

225. (A) A quota will increase the price of foreign imported rice. Consumers may start to buy other starches to substitute for rice.

226. (B) Choice B is the best answer because it is the only answer that illustrates the purpose of a tariff: a tax placed on foreign goods as a way to protect domestic producers.

227. (D) A protective tariff is an excise tax levied on importation of a foreign good that is also produced in the domestic market. A protective tariff increases the price of foreign products, thereby protecting the domestic industry from global competition.

228. (E) An import quota sets a maximum number of goods that can be imported into the domestic market. A quota does not collect revenue for the government.

229. (A) Choice A is the best answer because if a nation's currency depreciates, domestic goods become less expensive to foreign consumers.

230. (B) When a nation's currency falls or weakens in price relative to another currency, it has depreciated. In the case of this question, fewer U.S. dollars would be needed to buy Japanese yen.

231. (E) When a nation buys a foreign company, real estate, or the financial assets of another nation, these transactions appear in the capital account of the balance of payments statement.

232. (C) The law of comparative advantage states that countries benefit by trading goods they can produce at low opportunity costs for goods that would incur higher opportunity costs to produce.

233. (D) The law of comparative advantage states that countries benefit by trading goods they can produce at low opportunity costs for goods that would incur higher opportunity costs to produce. Choice D is the best answer because each country should produce its good at a lower opportunity cost than the other.

234. (A) Choice B is incorrect because the Federal Reserve does not influence the exchange rate nor does it have the power to. Choice C is incorrect because fiscal policy is the powers of the government to stimulate the economy through taxing and spending. Choice D is incorrect because a balance of payments records payments between the United States and foreign countries. Choice E is incorrect because a protective tariff is a tax on foreign goods. Choice A is the best answer because the best exchange rate reflects an unregulated market dictated by supply and demand.

235. (A) Balance of payments is calculated by adding the current account and the capital account. A floating exchange rate is calculated through the market forces of supply and demand. A fixed exchange rate is established by a nation's government to another country's currency or the price of gold. The rate of inflation may be calculated by subtracting real income from nominal income.

236. (D) If the value of a nation's currency rises in relation to another nation's currency, it appreciated in value.

237. (A) If the value of a nation's currency falls in relation to another nation's currency, it depreciated in value.

238. (A) The Smoot-Hawley Act dramatically increased tariffs on foreign goods during the Great Depression. The goal was to protect American farmers, which then spread to other sectors of the U.S. economy. Other countries retaliated by increasing their taxes on imported goods. This severely worsened the effects of the Great Depression throughout the world.

239. (A) Choice A is the best answer because a nation will always have a trade surplus if the number of exports is higher than the number of imports. Choice B is incorrect because it reflects a trade deficit. Choices C and D are incorrect because these forces would not ensure a trade surplus. Choice E is incorrect because if the U.S. dollar appreciates relative to another nation's currency, it would make U.S. goods more expensive and the number of exports would decrease.

240. (D) A current account shows payments on imports and exports of goods and services and investment income sent abroad and received by the United States. If the foreign currency entering exceeds the amount of dollars exiting the United States, it is said to be a negative current account.

241. (C) The answer to this question is very self-explanatory. Domestic prices are used for trade within a country, when there is no need to use world prices. When a country engages in trade with another country, world prices are used.

242. (D) The definition of capital account is the flow of investment on real or financial assets between a nation and foreigners. Choices A and B are incorrect because they refer to methods to protect domestic producers. Choice C is incorrect, although subtracting the current account from the capital account equals the balance of payments. Choice E is incorrect because it refers to setting the world price of goods.

243. (A) If consumers have a stronger preference for foreign-made goods, the demand for the foreign nation's currency increases and the dollar depreciates. This would affect the exchange rate. If a nation's economy is growing, incomes tend to rise. If incomes are increasing, then consumption is increasing as well, thus affecting the appreciation of currency, which would in turn affect the exchange rate.

244. (A) If aggregate supply increases, the global value of that currency decreases. More of that nation's currency is needed to purchase another country's currency, thus affecting the exchange rate.

245. (B) Choice B is the best answer because if a nation's currency appreciates (rises in value), more money is needed to purchase that nation's goods. This would result in a decrease in that nation's exports.

246. (B) Choice E is not related to the arguments supporting NAFTA. Choice B is the best answer because nations choose to specialize and trade based on comparative advantage or low opportunity costs. Choices A and C are incorrect because they are negative arguments against NAFTA.

247. (C) Choices A and B may be eliminated because they refer to economic organizations beyond the Western Hemisphere. Choice D is incorrect because it increased the severity of the Great Depression throughout the world. Choice E is incorrect because it was enacted in the 1930s but the question is asking for economic integration in recent years. NAFTA began in 1994.

248. (A) Choice A is the best answer because market fluctuations may affect the exchange rate, which is based on supply and demand. Although a fixed exchange rate is the most efficient, it may be the most volatile due to market fluctuations.

249. (A) Choice A is the best answer because more of a foreigner's currency is needed to purchase U.S. dollars. Choices B and C are incorrect because a strong dollar would have more purchasing power in a foreign country. Choice D is incorrect because a fixed exchange rate cannot be hurt or helped, as it is dependent upon another nation's currency. Choice E is incorrect because competition among two foreign nations is not affected by the U.S. dollar, but only by their own respective currencies.

250. (A) Choice A is the best answer because a strong dollar would have more purchasing power in a foreign country.